Let's have a little quiz:

1. Who meets there?
2. What do they do there?
3. Do they help you in any way?

If your answers were:

1. "Members of the government"
2. "They represent all the people living in the country."
3. "Yes, they create laws to protect me and my family."

Then let me congratulate you on getting every one of your answers wrong.

Didn't do too well on that quiz? OK, let's have another go:

4. When was slavery abolished?
5. Was slavery legal?
6. Are you in debt to a financial institution?

Here are the answers:

1. The serving officers of a commercial corporation.
2. They think up ways to take money and goods from you.
3. No, absolutely not, they help themselves and not you.

4. Slavery has NEVER been abolished and you yourself are considered to be a slave right now.
5. Yes, slavery is "legal" although it is not "lawful" (you need to discover the difference).
6. No. You are NOT in debt to any financial institution.

Does this seem a little strange to you? If it does, then read on:

THOSE IN POWER HAVE A BIG SECRET

- **Paying tax is OPTIONAL !!**
- **Registering a vehicle is OPTIONAL !!**
- **Paying a fine is OPTIONAL !!**
- **Attending a court is OPTIONAL !!**

YOU CAN IF YOU WANT TO, BUT YOU DON'T HAVE TO.
Surprised? Well – try this on for size:

Every Mortgage and Loan is FULLY REPAID from day one – you can pay it again if you want to, but you don't have to !!

If nobody has told that you have a Strawman, then this could be a very interesting experience for you.

Your Strawman was created when you were very young, far too young to know anything about it. But then, it was meant to be a secret as its purpose is to swindle you, and it has been used very effectively to do just that ever since it was created.

Perhaps it is about time that you learned about your Strawman and how you can stop it being used against you. Knowing about it is the most important first step. You need to go on a journey of discovery, and I'm afraid that what you are about to discover is not very pleasant. However, if you decide to act on what you learn, it could change your life for the better.

If you think that you are in debt, then you can get out of it if you are willing to stand up for your rights and refuse to be swindled any longer.

Interested? If so, then let's start at the beginning and find out where your Strawman came from — and why you should care about it.

It all started when your parents had a happy event and you entered the world. You don't know exactly when that was, because you were not aware of the days of the week, the months of the year, or even what year it was. Even after some months had gone by, you still were not aware of these things, but by that time, your Strawman had already been created, and it was being used to make some very unscrupulous people rich.

None of this was your fault. It happened because your parents were fooled into thinking that they needed to register your birth and get a birth certificate for you. So, they APPLIED for a birth certificate, not understanding what would happen when they did.

Well then, what did happen? According to the Local Authority:

1. They lost ownership of their baby (you).
2. They allowed a Strawman to be created.

This is not something which they can be blamed for, as nobody told them it would, or even could, happen. Nor did anybody tell your parents what a Strawman is or how it can be used against their baby. In actual fact, the "registration" is a contract which is, in reality, null and void because there was no full disclosure by the Local Authority, nor was there 'intent to contract' on the part of your parents.

The registering of a baby's birth passes "ownership" of the baby to the Local Authority and that, and that alone, allows the Local Authority to take the child away from the parents if they ever want to do that. This applies until the child reaches the "age of maturity" set by the current legal statutes. Doing that is not "lawful" but after the birth has been registered, it is "legal" and there is a world of difference between those two terms, a difference which it is very important that you come to clearly understand.

So, What is a Strawman?

A Strawman is a fictitious legal entity, created with the hope that as the child grows up, he will be fooled into believing that he is actually the Strawman (which he most definitely is not) and pay all sorts of imaginary costs and liabilities which get attached to the Strawman by con artists.

How is a Strawman Created?

Well the mechanism involves that unnecessary birth certificate which the parents imagine is about, and belongs to, their baby (neither of which is actually true). If the baby has been named 'James' and the family name is 'Martin', then you would expect the birth certificate to have the name 'James Martin' printed on it. If that is what is printed on it, then all is well and it is a genuine birth certificate and nothing more. However, if any other name is there, then the document is not a birth certificate but instead is the creation of a Strawman masquerading as James Martin. The alternative entries might be any of the following examples: "JAMES MARTIN", "Mr. James Martin", "Martin, Mr. James" or anything else which is not exactly "James Martin" and nothing else.

Why Create a Strawman?

The answer is "in order to charge the Strawman imaginary costs and penalties and fool the human James Martin into paying those amounts". These imaginary charges include 'Income Tax', 'Council Tax', 'Inheritance Tax', 'Capital-Gains Tax', 'Road Tax', 'Import Tax', 'Value-Added Tax', 'Fuel Levy', 'Loan Interest', 'Bank Charges' and anything else that full-time professionals can think up and are confident that you will not notice that you never agreed to pay, and don't need to pay.

"Legalese"

"Legalese" is a secret language invented to trick you. It uses English words but attaches secret meanings to those words with the sole intention of stopping you from believing that what they are saying to you has nothing to do with the normal meaning in the English language. Their purpose is to cheat you and rob you.

For example, they will ask to you *"Do you understand?"*

In English, that means "Do you comprehend what I am saying to you?" And the automatic response would be "Yes", meaning "I do comprehend what you are saying to me". But these sneaky, underhand people have changed the meaning in Legalese to mean "Do you stand under me?" meaning "Do you grant me authority over you so that you have to obey whatever I tell you to do?"

What makes it even worse, is the fact that they will never tell you that they have switched from English to Legalese, and if that is not dishonest, underhand and unscrupulous, then I don't know what is! If you answer the question believing that English is being spoken, then they *pretend* that you are contracting with them to become subordinate to them. Whether or not that is actually true is debatable because that is effectively a verbal contract between you and them, and for any contract to be valid, there has to be full and open disclosure of all of the terms of the contract, and then, unreserved acceptance by both parties, and in these cases, that has most definitely, not occurred.

But what is the point in all this? Well, this manoeuvre is intended to trick you into agreeing to represent your Strawman. Why? Aaah, now, that's a good question, but to answer it takes a bit of explaining, and you need to understand the overall situation:

All humans are born equal, with complete freedom of choice and action. If you live in the same place as a lot of other people, then there are a few restrictions which have grown up, by common consent, over time. These restrictions are for your protection and the protection of the other people living near you. These restrictions are called "the Law" (or more accurately: "Common Law") and they are few in number and very easy to understand. They are:

1. You must not injure or kill anyone.

2. You must not steal or damage things owned by somebody else.

3. You must be honest in your dealings and not swindle anyone.

These restrictions have resulted from hundreds of years of disputes which have been dealt with through using common sense and the opinions of ordinary people. They are the only limitations on you, and if you don't want to abide by them, then you need to go to some isolated place, and stay away from other people.

Many people think that there are hundreds of other laws which they have to keep (and new ones every other day), but that is not so. Those other things are called "statutes" and keeping them is optional for you, the human, BUT they are NOT optional for your fictitious Strawman, and that is why the people who benefit from those things want to persuade you to represent your Strawman and so become subject to all of their invented restrictions and charges.

If you knew that they were optional, would you agree to:

1. Give most of your earnings away in taxes and similar charges?

2. Pay to own a vehicle?

3. Pay to own a television set?

4. Pay to drive on roads which were built with your money?

5. Be forced to join the armed services if you are told to?

6. Send an army which is supposed to represent you, into another country to murder innocent people there?

Were you ever told that these things are optional? If you agree to represent your Strawman, then these things become binding on you. These are some of the "statutes" which 'politicians' keep inventing in order to make you poor, make them and their friends rich, and keep you in a position where you have to do everything they say, no matter how much that harms you and does away with your natural freedom and rights.

But, says somebody, we elect a government to represent us and so we have to do what they say; after all, they have our best interests at heart; don't they?

Well, that is a nice thought, but is it actually true? No it isn't. You think that you elect politicians to represent you in your government, but that is not what you actually do.

That is part of a very carefully fostered *illusion* intended to keep you in your place and giving most of your earnings away (typically, 80% of all you earn). Part of the secret is that what is supposed to be your 'government' is actually a privately owned, for-profit company and all that you do when voting, is to help choose the serving officers inside that company. It will never make the slightest difference to what happens in the future as the company policy and actions are controlled by the owners of the company and they are not influenced in any way whatsoever by what you want.

Think this is far fetched? Then check it out via Dun & Bradstreet or any of the other place which records the setting up and performance of the 160,000,000 commercial companies world-wide. When you do that, you will discover, for example, that the United States is a commercial for-profit company.

The United States Corporation is a private company.

The non-federal Federal Reserve Bank is a private company set up in the year 1913, as is every Court and every Police Force and even Congress is a company and not a person.

Just in case you are not aware of it, the purpose of any commercial 'for-profit' company or corporation is to make money for its owners (and shareholders if there are any). The people who you think of as 'The Government' don't do anything that earns money - they instead take money from you, and their main job is to make sure that you don't realize that they are in the same position as IBM which takes away millions of your money every year.

So, why all the pretence of there being a genuine government which you elect and who serves you? They don't want you to understand that they are just running a company which produces nothing of any worth - something like a betting shop, where almost every customer loses money - and wake up to the fact that, unlike what you have been told all your life, this is all optional and you don't need to play their rip-off game any longer, unless you want to.

They want you to be so burdened down with paying them money and working so hard and so long that you don't have the time, money or energy to stop and think about what is happening to you and your family.

They are desperate to stop you from just walking away from their scam, so they make every effort to connect you with the fiction which is your Strawman because fictitious entities like commercial companies can't have any dealing with a real man or a real woman - they can only deal with another fiction like your Strawman, and it is essential that they fool you into believing that you have to act on behalf of your Strawman - which you don't.

They have a number of well-proven methods of distracting you and keeping you from finding out. They want you to see a great deal of entertainment, not because there is anything wrong with entertainment, but while you are being entertained you will not be asking awkward questions. Also, they are very careful that most entertainment reinforces their make-believe world and makes it appear to be "the real world" where everyone is under 'The Government', Police Officers uphold the law, taxes are essential in order to keep things going, and things which are said to be bad for you, are taxed heavily (not to make money) but supposedly, to encourage you to avoid those things. You will notice that they keep saying that their invented "statutes" are "the law" which they most certainly are not, but if they say it often enough, people start believing it and never think to question what they say.

They also have another very effective technique, and that is

FEAR. They want you to be afraid. Afraid of imaginary terrorists. Afraid of disasters. Afraid of new diseases. Afraid of foreign countries. Afraid of "the economy" doing badly and inflation rising. If you doubt this, then take a look at the news and count the number of positive, uplifting news items, and the number of negative or depressing news items. It doesn't take much in the way of research to see the very heavy negative bias in the news. The reason behind this is to make you feel that you need a   Government and an Army to protect you from these supposed dangers. It is easy to keep the news items biased that way, because all of the major news agencies and media outlets in the world are owned by only five or six privately owned commercial companies.

So to supposedly connect you to the Strawman which they created for you when your birth was registered, they use the Legalese technique of conning you with the Name of the Strawman. If you are ill-advised enough to go to a Court (which is a Corporate place of Business) as "the accused", you will be asked to confirm your name, quoting the full name shown on your birth certificate, which is the LEGAL PERSONALITY. Titles such as Mr., Dr., Rev., Gov., Sec., or whatever are not asked for as they are not required. The "Accused" is actually the LEGAL PERSONALITY which is the name on the birth certificate, so when they ask for the person's NAME, they are talking to the LEGAL PERSONALITY (the Strawman) and not to the human. This is because a human cannot exist in the legal world - only pieces of paper can, and that is something which they are very careful not to tell you.

This is a really Key issue. Natural Law and Common Law are the only laws which apply to humans and they deal only with harming other people or causing them loss, and outside of those restrictions, a human has free and unlimited entitlement to do anything he chooses which complies with these principles. As opposed to this, Acts of Congress, "Statutes" and Statutory Instrument "Contracts" do not apply to the human but only to the piece of paper which is the LEGAL PERSONALITY which has no reality. As the legal fiction—the LEGAL PERSONALITY— was created by the company called "THE UNITED STATES

CORPORATION", that company gets to say what the rights and duties for that piece of paper are.

When a person is born in America, the mother and father submit a Birth Certificate Registration Form, which is a piece of paper. There is no requirement under common law to do this. When any limited company or corporation is set up, there is always a Certificate of Registration in order to create its LEGAL PERSON-ALITY, and that is a piece of paper. Please note that an American Birth Certificate states quite clearly that it is not evidence of identity, meaning that, it has nothing to do with any human. Marked on it is "U.S. Copyright" showing clearly that it does not belong to an individual and was created by the State. This act of Registering a child, makes that child a "ward of the court" and the child can be taken away from the parents at any time.

The Legalese definitions of words which sound commonplace, can be found in Black's Law Dictionary and the current edition is the eighth.

Interestingly, in Legalese, you the human are defined as a "monster" which shows exactly what the people who use Legalese think of you - charming people aren't they?

Another trick they try to play on you is to imply that a Summons is something which you MUST obey while in fact, it is only an Invitation to attend their place of business. They are NOT inviting you the man or woman, but instead, they are inviting the LEGAL PERSONALITY to their place of business, and please note that there is a CHOICE, as it is only an invitation.

The LEGAL PERSONALITY is just a piece of paper, a BIRTH CERTIFICATE created by the commercial company called "The United States Corporation", and it is not the human. You can't be forced into a contract, so they have to deceive you into entering into one without understanding what you are doing. They are using deception as every Judge's Court is a trading name of the commer-cial company called "The Department of Justice" which does not have a Parent Company listed, meaning that it is a Parent Company itself. Legal people, on being shown this company registration, respond by realizing that if this information is genuine (which it is) then the US has been lawless for more than 100 years because the whole Justice System is being dealt with by a commercial company.

Going to court in connection with any civil action is a very bad idea as the only function of a court is to judge between two parties who disagree and then penalize the loser. The court doesn't care who wins or loses, and the objective of the court is to make a profit for its owners as it is a commercial enterprise and its purpose is to acquire money from anybody who is foolish enough to attend. If you look at the Summons (which is really an invitation to go to court), you will see that it is not in your name, but in the name of the Strawman which they are hoping to fool you into representing.

DEALING WITH DEBT

Because of the very high percentage of the money earned being taken away from the average person, it is not unusual for people to end up with what looks like "debt". Most people spend their time worrying over the statement of what they are told they owe, and do endless calculations to see if they agree with the numbers which they have been sent. Again, this is the sort of misdirection which magicians use to fool audiences, distracting their attention away from where the action is really taking place. Here, the question is really not "How much is owed?" But instead is "Is anything *actually* owed?"

You need to remember that any financial institution is a legal fiction and does not actually exist. As a result of this, it can only deal with other legal fictions (essentially, other pieces of paper) and it can't have any dealings with a man or a woman as they are not legal fictions. It is also important to understand what passes for money nowadays. Let's say our trusty friend James Martin goes looking for a loan and he fills out an application form with the Swindle Bank, Inc. for $10,000. Interestingly, the form which he is asked to sign, says that he has already received the $10,000 although the loan has not yet been approved.

The next day, the loan is approved and James is handed a check which he is asked to sign and deposit to his account with the bank. We won't follow up on that very interesting procedure at this time, but please remember that he has now provided *two signatures* for $10,000 in the Strawman name, and all he has received is a '1' and four zeros in the accounts of the Swindle Bank.

All goes well for several months until James loses his job and does not manage to get another one. This is financial trouble which he does not know how to deal with. Time goes by and James has not had sufficient money to make payments against his loan from the Swindle Bank Inc. He starts getting letters from the bank saying that he must pay the arrears immediately and keep up with the payments in future. There is not the slightest chance of that happening as James just does not have the money and he does not know what to do.

Fortunately, Peter, the next door neighbor of James, happens to be an independent financial advisor with years of experience, and James has the idea of asking him for help. Peter is willing to help and so he sits down and goes through all of the paperwork.

Then he tells James: "You must not ignore this situation. Write back immediately and say that you agree to pay any financial obligation which you might lawfully owe, ON THE CONDITION that they provide:

1. Validation of the debt—that is, the actual accounting.

2. Verification of their claim against you; that is, a signed Invoice.

3. A copy of the Contract binding both parties (you and them), in a letter by 'certified mail' so that there is an independent "witness to it having been delivered."

Every letter you write should be marked clearly *"__Without Prejudice__"* which means that you reserve all your lawful rights and you accept no contract unless it is shown to be lawful by meeting the four essential conditions to a lawful binding contract— namely:

1. Full Disclosure (you were not told that you were actually creating the credit with your wet ink signature);

2. Equal Consideration (they brought nothing of value to the table and so had nothing to lose);

3. Lawful Terms and Conditions (your's were based on fraud);

4. The wet ink signatures of both parties — (corporations can't sign because they have no Right or Mind to contract since they are soul-less legal fictions; and furthermore, no third party can sign a contract on their behalf).

Peter then tells James that agreeing to pay provided that evidence of a lawful debt can be produced, stops him being taken to court because courts only adjudicate between parties who are in dispute, and as James has agreed to pay there is no dispute, so the court would not accept any application for a hearing. If the Swindle Bank were foolish enough to try, James has only to send the court a copy of his letter agreeing to pay, and the case would be thrown out (dismissed) immediately (and the Bank might well be penalized for wasting the court's time).

The bank is now in trouble as it has been running a con game on James and so can't produce the documents, for which James has asked. The request by James was reasonable in every respect. However, a loan agreement is a contract and so there has to be full disclosure of all the details (which there wasn't), both sides have to put up something of equal worth (which didn't happen), and the contract has to be signed in wet ink by both parties (which the bank can't do). So the bank has a real problem.

The bank will probably send a Statement of what it wants James to believe is the outstanding amount. James should return this with a polite note saying that a 'Statement' is not an 'Invoice', so would they please provide a signed 'Invoice' as requested. They will also probably send a photocopy of his Loan Application form, at which point James should write back and point out politely that it does not constitute a contract as it is only signed by one of the parties (himself) and he has asked for a copy of the Contract signed by both parties.

The bank is likely to go silent at this point and stop corresponding with James. James should then write again, requesting that the necessary documents be sent to him within the next fourteen (or perhaps 28) days, and if that does not happen, then he will consider the debt to be fully discharged.

The bank will either remain silent or write back to say that the debt is fully discharged. If the bank tries phoning, then just tell them politely that you only wish to deal with this matter in writing, and hang up. If the bank remains silent for the stated period of time, then James should write back stating that due to the bank's failure to provide the necessary evidence of a lawful debt within the reasonable period of time provided, that James now considers that the debt is fully discharged, and ask the bank to confirm that in writing. The bank will normally write back confirming that the debt is fully discharged and that there is nothing owing and if it does not do that, it will just stop asking for any further payments.

The reasons for how and why this takes place, takes a good deal of explaining and many people find it difficult to understand. So it is covered in detail on the following pages here. Many people think that this process sounds like you ripping off the bank, but this is definitely not the case.

WHAT IS MONEY?

Originally, in England, the unit of money was called "one pound sterling". That was because it was literally, sterling silver weighing one pound. As it was quite difficult to carry several pounds weight of currency around with you, it was arranged that the actual silver could be held in a bank and a promissory note which was essentially, a receipt for the deposit of each pound of silver on deposit, was issued. It was much easier to carry these "bank notes" around and to do business with them. If you wanted to, you could always take these notes to a bank and ask for them to be cashed, and the bank would hand you the equivalent weight of sterling silver in exchange for the notes.

Today, the currency in America is "bank notes" which are certainly easier to carry around than metal coins, but there is one very important difference. These notes are issued by the private company called "The Federal Reserve Bank" (which is as good a name for a company as any other name). However, if you were to take one of their bank notes to a branch of that company and ask for it to be cashed, all that they would do is give you *another* note with the same numbers of credit printed on it, or alternatively, other notes with smaller numbers printed on them. This is because, unlike the *original* bank notes, there is nothing of any physical value backing up the bank notes of today - they are only materially worth the physical paper on which they are printed.

It actually gets worse than that. What happens most commonly nowadays is that they do not even bother printing those pieces of paper. Now, they just tap some numbers into a computer record, or if they are old-fashioned enough, they write the numbers into a ledger by hand. What do those numbers represent? Nothing at all - they have no actual value, in other words, just as much value as if you typed them into your own computer - quite meaningless - and yet, a bank or other financial institution will merrily "lend" you those numbers in return for years of your work, plus interest charges — now isn't that really generous of them?

Actually, this is not at all funny, because if you don't keep paying them money earned by your very real work, they will attempt to take your house and possessions away from you. This won't happen if you understand that what they lent you was actually valueless. Take the case of Jerome Daly of Minnesota in America. In court, Jerome challenged the right of the bank to foreclose on his home which had been purchased with a loan from the bank. Jerome argued that any mortgage contract required that both parties (that is, himself and the bank) put up a legitimate form of property for the exchange. In legal language, that is called a legitimate "consideration" put forward by both parties to the contract.

Jerome explained that the "money" was in fact not the property of the bank as it had been created out of nothing as soon as the loan agreement was signed. That is, the money does not come out of the bank's existing assets as the bank is simply inventing it, and in reality the bank is putting up nothing of its own, except for a fictional liability on paper. As the court case progressed, the President of the bank, Mr. Morgan, took the stand and admitted that the bank, in combination with the (privately owned commercial company called) "The Federal Reserve Bank", created the entire amount of the loan in "credit" in its own books by means of a book-keeping entry, the money and credit coming into existence when they created it. Further, Mr. Morgan admitted that no United States Law or Statute exists which gives him the right to do this. A lawful consideration must exist and must be tendered to support the loan agreement. The jury found that there had been no lawful consideration put forward by the bank, so the court rejected the bank's application for foreclosure and Jerome Daly kept his home debt free.

That is exactly the situation with all American mortgages. When someone makes an application for a mortgage or any other loan, the applicant's signature is required on the application form before the loan is approved. The "signature" on that signed application makes it a valuable piece of paper which the bank can deposit in its accounts as a credit to the bank for the amount of the loan. The bank could just keep that application form and stay ahead by $100,000 or whatever, but they want more, much more. They want the borrower to pay them that same amount again, funding it by years of labor, and not only the amount of the supposed "loan" but significant extra amount in interest as well. Why do you think that they are so keen to lend you "money" - they are even willing to lend to people with very poor credit, as there is no way that the bank can lose out on the deal, no matter what happens.

This is why, if a company starts demanding payment of large sums of money, you start by asking them to provide the "accounting" for the deal. In other words, you are asking them to show in writing that they provided something of genuine worth as their side of the loan contract. As they invented the money as numbers in their books, with no real worth attached to those numbers, they are in deep trouble as they can't comply with your demand to see their accounting for the deal. Did you ever wonder how the average bank manages to make hundreds of millions of dollars profit every year?

Well, you are looking right at where a large chunk of it comes from.

THE BOOKKEEPING

This next part of the information may be a little difficult to understand. When any business is being run, the accounts are recorded as money "coming in" and money "going out". For a bank, the money coming in is called a "Credit" and money going out is called a "Debit". The objective is to have these two amounts always match each other (balance) for any customer. Not everything done in banking is immediately obvious to the average person, so it may be a little difficult to understand how everything works in this area.

If you have an account with a bank and you deposit $200 to open the account, the bank enters that in its books as a Credit. The Credit on your account is $200 and the Debit is $0, so the balance has a positive, or Credit, value of $200.

If you were to withdraw $300, then the bank would record this as a Debit of $300. When the Credit balance on your account is $200, the balance on your account would be $100 in Debit, that is, overdrawn by $100.

If you were to deposit a further $100 and then close your account, the bank would not have any problem, other than the fact that they would like to keep you on as a customer.

As far as the accounting goes, your account is balanced and the bank is satisfied with the state of affairs, $300 has come in and $300 has gone out, the books balance - case closed.

Now, if you were to apply for a loan (mortgage or otherwise) for $100,000 from the bank, they would give you an application form which is set out in such a way that you have to fill in the Strawman's name rather than your own - separate boxes with one of them containing "Mr." and they may even require you to fill the form in using block capital letters.

You may think that the capital letters are so that they can read you writing or perhaps, to make it easier for it to be entered into a computer, but the name in those capital letters belongs to the Strawman and not to you. You have actually just made an application on behalf of the Strawman and not on behalf of yourself!

You might wonder why they would want you to do this. After all, what could they ever get from the Strawman? Well, you might be surprised. When the Strawman was incorporated they assigned a large monetary value to it, possibly $100,000,000 and they have been trading on the stock market on behalf of the Strawman ever since, and you know how many years that has been. So, very surprisingly, in their opinion, the little fellow is really very rich, and you have just authorized them to take the amount of your loan application from the Strawman's account. So before the bank passes you any money, it has already gotten its money from the Strawman account and entered it in its books as a $100,000 Credit to your loan account. They then place $100,000 into your loan account as a Debit. Interestingly, that loan account is now balanced and could easily be closed off as a completed deal.

This is where the sneaky part comes in. To get the money out of your account, you have to write and sign a check for $100,000 on that account. What does the bank do with checks which you sign? It assigns them to the account as an asset of the bank, and suddenly, the bank is ahead by $100,000 because the check is in the name of the Strawman who can supply the bank with almost any amount of money. But it doesn't end there, as the bank is confident that you know so little about what is going on that you will pay them anything up to $100,000 over the years, against what you believe you owe them! If that happens, then they have made yet another $100,000 for the bank. To make things even better for them, they want you to pay them interest on the money which you (don't actually) owe them. Overall, they make a great deal of money when you borrow from them, so perhaps you can see now why banks make hundreds of millions in profit each year.

If the loan were used to buy a property, then the bank probably insisted that you assign the title deeds to them as collateral for the loan, as soon as the property deal closed (was completed). If you then fail to keep paying them, they are likely to attempt to foreclose on the "loan" and sell your property quickly for an even greater profit. And to add insult to injury, if the property sale did not exceed the amount of the "loan" plus the charges for selling it, then they are likely to claim that you owe them the difference!

Perhaps you can now see why Jerome Daly told them to go take a running jump at themselves, and why your request for "the accounting" for any loan made to you, puts the bank in an impossible situation. If the bank then just writes and tells you that the "debt" is fully discharged, they still have made a massive profit on the operation, and they also hope that the vast majority of their customers will not catch on to the fact that they are paying far too much for their property, or even that there is a Strawman involved.

Please don't feel that you are ripping off the banks if you don't pay them what they are asking you to pay - they have already recovered everything paid out before you start paying them for the second or third time.

When it is a Mortgage the entire process is very much the same. The "Debt-Free Sovereign" web site:

http://www.freewebs.com/debtfreesovereign gives a very clear description of this process in Canada, and the process is much the same everywhere else. They describe a typical property sale and mortgage this way:

The buyer goes to Magic Bank in response to the bank's claim that it is in the business of lending money in accordance with its corporate charter. The buyer went to the bank believing that Magic Bank had the asset (money) to lend. Magic Bank never tells its customers the truth that it does not have any money to lend, nor that Magic Bank is not permitted to use their depositors' money to lend to its borrowers.

Notwithstanding the fact that Magic Bank does not have any money to lend, Magic Bank makes the buyer/borrower sign a mortgage loan application form which is essentially a promissory note saying that the buyer/borrower promises to pay Magic Bank for the money (what money?) which he is supposed to receive from Magic Bank even before any value or consideration is received by the buyer/borrower from Magic Bank. This promissory note is a valuable consideration, a receivable, and therefore an asset transferred from the buyer to the bank which Magic Bank enters into its own asset account as a cash deposit.

After making sure that the buyer has the ability to pay the required monthly payments (the buyer has credit), Magic Bank agrees to lend the buyer the money (cash) to pay the seller. Magic Bank has no money to lend but it gave the buyer a promise to lend money by way of a commitment letter, loan approval letter, loan authorization, or loan confirmation letter, etc., signed by a bank official or loan/mortgage officer employed by Magic Bank.

Magic Bank's acceptance of the buyer's promissory note makes the bank liable to the buyer/borrower for the full face value of the promissory note which is the agreed purchase price of the property, less any cash deposit or down payment money paid by the buyer directly to the seller. It is important to note at this point that all real estate transactions require that the property being sold must be conveyed, by the seller to the buyer, free of all liens and encumbrances which means that all liens such as existing mortgages, judgments, etc. must be paid before the property can be mortgaged by the buyer as collateral to the mortgage loan which is yet to be received by the buyer pursuant to the promise made by Magic Bank. How can the seller pay off his mortgage and obtain clear title if he has not yet received any money from the buyer? And how can the buyer mortgage a property that does not yet belong to him?

This dilemma is solved using Magic Bank's magic bag of tricks. Magic Bank, in concert with the bank's lawyers, or notaries, causes all the liens and encumbrances to magically disappear by writing a

Magic Bank check, backed by the buyer's promissory note and agreement of purchase and sale, deposited into the lawyer's trust account, to pay the seller for the property at closing. In essence, using the buyer's promissory note as the cash to enable the agreement of purchase and sale.

So the buyer's promissory note made the conveyance possible. Magic Bank caused the property to be conveyed from the seller to the buyer with title free and clear of all encumbrances and liens. The property now belongs to the buyer which makes it possible for the buyer to mortgage his property to Magic Bank. The buyer actually paid for the property using his own promissory note.

At this point, the seller has not yet received any money or cash so Magic Bank and its magicians must perform more magic in order to satisfy the seller's requirement that he get paid, or the whole deal is null and void. The seller does not even know that the property has been magically conveyed to the buyer's name in order for the seller to receive any money.

The ensuing magic trick is accomplished this way. The buyer is made to sign *another* promissory note. The mortgage contract is attached to the promissory note which makes the buyer liable to pay Magic Bank for the money or the loan which the buyer has not yet or may never receive for up to twenty five years or more depending on the term of the mortgage contract. This note is linked to the collateral through the mortgage contract and as such, it is valuable to Magic Bank.

Magic Bank then goes to the Federal Reserve Bank or to another bank to pledge the deal that they have just gotten from the buyer for credit. The Federal Reserve Bank then gives Magic Bank the "credit". Remember, it is not Magic Bank's credit, it is the buyer's credit who promised to pay Magic Bank if and when the money is received by the buyer from Magic Bank, payable for up to 25 years or more.

Note: What happened above is basically a "swap" transaction all banks do to 'monetize' security. In this case, the second promissory note that is linked to the mortgage contract and signed by the buyer is a mortgage-backed security.

Magic Bank will then agree to pay the Federal Reserve Bank a certain percentage of interest over "prime". Thus the buyer's loan package goes to the Federal Reserve Bank which credits Magic Bank with the full amount of credit which is the total amount of the money Magic Bank is entitled to receive after 25 years which is the amount of the principal plus all the interest payments the buyer has promised to pay to Magic Bank for 25 years or more which is usually three times the amount of the money promised by Magic Bank to the buyer. By magic, Magic Bank just enriched itself and got paid in advance, without using or risking its own money.

Magic Bank's magician, the lawyer who holds the check that is backed by the buyer's original promissory note, then writes a check to the seller as payment for the property.

In effect, the buyer paid the seller with his own money by virtue of the fact that it was the buyer's own money (the promissory note) that made the purchase and sale possible.

Magic Bank just made a cool 300% profit without using or risking any capital of its own.

Neither was there any depositor's money deducted from Magic Bank's asset account in this transaction.

What really happened was pure deception and if we the people tried to do this, we would end up in prison being found guilty of fraud and criminal conversion not to mention that the property would have been seized by the court.

This is only a crime if we, the people, do it to each other, as it would be an indictable crime if we issued a check with no funds. There would not be any deal, no purchase and sale agreement because there is no valuable consideration. In order to de-criminalize the transaction, we need Magic Bank and their cohorts to make the deal happen. It is really a conspiracy of sorts but these "persons", the banks, the lawyers, the land title offices or even the courts do not consider the transaction as fraudulent transactions because these transactions happen all the time.

Such a contract is "void ab-initio" or "void from the beginning" which means that the contract never took place in the first place. Moreover, the good faith and fair dealing requirement through full disclosure is non-existent which further voids the contract.

Magic Bank failed to disclose to the buyer that it will not be giving the buyer any valuable consideration and taking interest back as additional benefit to unjustly enrich the corporation. Magic Bank also failed to disclose how much profit they are going to make on the deal.

Magic Bank led the buyer to believe that the money going to the seller would be coming from its own asset account. They lied because they knew, or ought to have known, that their own book or ledger would show that Magic Bank does not have any money to lend and that their records will show that no such loan transaction ever took place. Their own book will show that there would be no debits from Magic Bank's asset account at all and all that would show up are the two entries made when the buyer gave Magic Bank the first collateral or the promissory note which enabled Magic Bank to cut a check which made it possible to convey the property from seller to the buyer free and clear of all liens or encumbrances as required by the agreement of purchase and sale entered into in writing between the buyer and the seller. What really happened was not magic; in reality, the buyer's promissory note was used by Magic Bank and its magicians - the lawyers and land title clerks - to convey free title to the buyer from the seller. So why do we need the mortgage contract at all?

The other entry that would show up when we audit Magic Bank's accounts, is the other pledge of collateral including the buyer's promissory note which was converted (unlawfully and without disclosure or permission from the buyer) into a mortgage-backed security which was "swapped" or deposited by Magic Bank to the Federal Reserve Bank for which another deposit was entered into Magic Bank's transaction account.

From the above, we can list all the criminal acts perpetrated by Magic Bank:

1. The mortgage contract was "void ab-initio" because Magic Bank lied and never intended to lend a single cent of their own asset or depositor's money to the buyer.

2. A valid contract must have lawful or valuable consideration. The contract failed for anticipated breach. Magic Bank never planned to give the buyer/borrower any valuable consideration.

3. Magic Bank breached all its fiduciary duties to the buyer and is therefore guilty of criminal breach of trust by failing in its good faith requirement.

4. Magic Bank concealed the fact from the buyer that it would be using the buyer's promissory notes; first to clear all the liens and encumbrances in order to convey clear title to the buyer and then use the second promissory note to obtain more money from the Federal Reserve Bank or other institutions that buy and sell mortgage-backed security. Magic Bank received up to three times the amount of money required to purchase the property and kept the proceeds to itself without telling the buyer.

5. Magic Bank violated its corporate charter by lending "credit" or "nothing at all" to the buyer and then charging interests on this make-believe loan. Banks are only licensed to lend their own money, not other people's money. Magic Bank used the buyer's promissory note to clear the title which essentially purchased the property from the seller. The transaction is "an ultra vires" transaction because Magic Bank has engaged in a contract "outside of it's lawful mandate". An ultra vires contract is void or voidable because it is non-existent in law.

6. Everyone involved in this undertaking with Magic Bank, starting with the loan or mortgage officer, the lawyers, the land title office and even the central bank are equally guilty by association by aiding and abetting Magic Bank in its commission of its crimes against the buyer and the people who would eventually have to absorb all of the loss through

increased taxes, etc.

In the final analysis, Magic Bank and the others who profited from the ultra vires transaction are all guilty of unjust enrichment and fraud for deceiving the buyer and the people, and for acting in concert in this joint endeavour to deceive the buyer.

DEALING WITH THE POLICE

Years ago, a policeman was your friend and defender. Things have changed now that Police Forces have become commercial organizations, dedicated to producing a profit by taking money from you in the form of Speeding Fines, Parking Fines and any number of other charges. It was stated on national TV recently that in the last thirteen years, three thousand additional offences have been invented.

As each individual Police Force is a commercial company, in a way like a McDonald's Restaurant in strategy, it has no authority to enforce anything, any more than a McDonald's has. The men and women who work under the banner of their local Police Force have two separate roles. When they take up their occupation, they take an oath of office, pledging to uphold the law.

That oath, and nothing else, gives them the authority to act to enforce Common Law - that is, the few things which are listed near the start of the "Legalese" section above. It does not authorize them to do anything connected with so-called "government" statutes, so they have been trained to use Legalese to entrap uninformed members of the public. To be fair, it is highly likely that members of the police force are not aware of what they are doing and do not understand the difference between "legal" statutes (which are optional) and the "lawful" Common Law requirements which apply to everyone and are not optional.

Please don't get me wrong. Most policemen and policewomen do a great job and assist members of the public, often above and beyond the requirements of their job - opposing bullying, intimidation, fraud, etc. and comforting in cases of bereavement or injury.

Admittedly, the commercial companies who control the Police Forces are working hard to end this sort of positive behavior, using ridiculous "Health and Safety" regulations as an excuse, even to the extent that police officers are instructed to stand by and watch somebody drown and not attempt to save them. This is not the choice of the officer but the instructions of the owners of the company.

Because these thousands of invented offences don't apply to anybody unless they agree to be bound by them, it becomes essential for a police officer to (possibly inadvertently) persuade a member of the public to agree to subject himself to these unnecessary restrictions and agree to pay invented cash penalties to the local commercial company called the "Police Force". The normal first attempt to establish this spurious dominance of the police officer is by him asking for your name. This is not an innocent question and it is essential that you are careful in what you say as there are Legalese booby traps all over the place.

One suitable reply is *"The law does not require me to provide that information"* which is entirely correct and avoids pitfall number one, and no matter how often the question is asked, the answer is always the same. *It is important not to argue with a police officer* as that is another Legalese booby trap which makes you subject to the thousands of hateful regulations designed to part you from your money. So, only answer questions, ideally, with a non-aggressive question, and don't volunteer any information.

If the police officer says *"You were exceeding the speed limit"*, you could say *"Was I?"* As you don't argue, nor do you say that the Common Law does not require anyone to keep to speed limits, obey road signs, park only where directed, etc. even though that is perfectly true. **Maxim: "Arguments are for fools".**

As mentioned before, if the police officer asks *"Do you understand?"* Your response should be *"No! — I do NOT <u>stand under you</u> in this matter".* As before, the question is a Legalese trap and has nothing whatsoever to do with understanding anything which has been said.

Under Common Law, an offense has only been committed if there is a victim (somebody who has been injured or killed, had possessions damaged or stolen, or who has been defrauded). So, if the police officer keeps pushing you to agree to pay his company money, when you don't need to, then a good question to ask might be *"Who is the victim?"* An alternative is to ask *"What is the charge or am I free to go?"* If you stick to these things, then the police officer has nothing to work on as you have not agreed to be bound by statutes; you have not provided a name and address for him to write on an Invoice (or "Fixed Penalty Notice" as they like to call it) and you have not entered into a "controversy" by arguing with him, or into "dishonor" by refusing him point blank.

There is one other thing, and that is, without being aggressive or offensive in any way, you must not DO anything which he tells you to do because if you do, then those charming Legalese people can see that you agree to "stand under" him and become subject to his "legal" (but not "lawful") authority, and so become liable to those thousands of cunning plans called "statutes", carefully crafted in order to rob you in a perfectly "legal" but not "lawful" way.

One thing which any police officer needs to become aware of is the fact that they do not have any security provided by the Police Force which employs them. In any situation which does not involve Common Law, the police officer is on his own, acting as an individual contractor and as such is wide open to action against him either under Common Law if he is acting unlawfully or by civil court action if his actions warrant it. If there is failure to establish "Joinder" (which is where a human voluntarily agrees to represent the Strawman and so become subject to statutes), then the presumed authority of a police officer does not exist in any respect and he is acting solely as an individual whose only authority is to enforce Common Law and nothing else.

REGISTRATION

Most people believe that when they buy a new car that they have to register it with the commercial company known as the

"Department of Motor Vehicles". What very few people are aware of is the fact that the act of applying for registration confirms the transfers the physical ownership of the vehicle from you the purchaser who paid the money, to the State. That is, you have given the vehicle away to a commercial company who has done nothing at all for you and which does not have your best interests at heart. Since it is unlawful to swindle anyone, I would be most interested to hear any reason why this registration should not be deemed to be unlawful, blatant, and an obvious fraud, for there has not been full disclosure of the silent and adhesive contract terms.

The change of ownership is shown by the fact that you, the previous owner, are now sent a document stating that your Straw-man is now the "Registered Owner" of the vehicle which you have just bought. You are left to pay for maintaining the vehicle which you do not own, and which the actual owner will, seize and sell the vehicle (which cost him nothing) if you, as agent for the "Registered Owner" do not keep on paying for the use of the vehicle.

Seizing the vehicle would not be lawful if the vehicle did not belong to the company doing the seizing.

The vehicle will be seized if the "Registration Tax" is not paid. That "tax" was originally introduced as a fund contributed to by the vehicle drivers, in order to build new roads, and to maintain roads that exist. That was a reasonable idea which means that all the roads in the country belong to the people who paid the money for them to be built and repaired.

Local Authorities say that they can't maintain roads properly as they do not have sufficient funds to do the work. The charge is more for vehicles of larger size on the excuse that they burn more fuel and so contribute more to global warming. The real purpose for the increase is to take more money from people who have no idea what is going on. There is even a proposal now, that motorists be charged for every mile that they drive along the roads which they paid for and own.

That, of course, is not the only stream of income from vehicles.

A major source of income is from the massive "tax" on fuel for vehicles, and it has been stated that an incredible 65% of the selling price is the proportion which is not needed for the location, extraction, processing and delivery of the actual fuel. In passing it can be noted that vehicles can be run on water, compressed air, energy direct from the environment, permanent magnets, and even on gravity. It will, without doubt, be a shock to you that many of the inventors who have done this suddenly disappeared as soon as they started testing their prototypes. Far fetched? I know of five people who have been told to "cease and desist - or else". When you understand the billions and billions in profit that are made through selling oil products, actions like that become very understandable, especially since the people who do these things own the police forces and the courts, and know that there will be no comeback no matter what they do.

So, what about the Driver's License? Under Common Law, humans have the right to travel freely and that includes using a vehicle when travelling. The Legalese people want to persuade you that you are no longer a "Traveller" under Common Law, but instead, you are a "Driver" subject to their statutes, and they demand that a "Driver" must have a driver's licence, registration tax, car insurance, and anything else that they can think up. If you wish to live in freedom and somebody asks to see your licence, then the question is "Why would I want one of those?"

A driver's licence is only needed for the driver of a vehicle which is being used in commerce. It can be argued that transporting a Strawman is a commercial undertaking, so it would be advisable to not have anything related to a Strawman with you on the road. It is also important to not give your name, address or (supposed) date of birth or to show any form of ID as that places you in a position of voluntarily submission by:

(a) Obeying the command of another human being (who is of equal standing to you);

(b) Associating yourself with, and consequently representing, a Strawman who is automatically subject to all statutes, being itself, a legal fiction joined to that fictional world.

So, if you are not carrying a passenger who is paying for the journey and you are not stopping off on the journey to sell things and you are not transporting a Strawman, then you are not a "Driver" with a "Passenger", but are instead a "Traveller", with a "Guest". Travellers do not need a driver's licence.

POSTAL DEMANDS

Each person generally gets a number of demands for amounts to be paid (Bills). If you get a demand for payment, you will notice that it is not addressed to you, the human, but to the fictional Strawman which has a name which sounds like your name but is not the same. The name will be printed on the demand in all capital letters, or in rare cases preceded by "Mr.", "Mrs." or "Miss.", and any one of those names refers to the Strawman who sounds like you and which has a creation date which matches what you have been told was your birthday. You can pay this demand if you want to, but it is entirely optional. Remember that it is not YOU who is being billed. Also worth remembering is that you, the human, are bound by Common Law and not legal statutes, and Common Law does not require you to pay any form of tax.

The company invoicing the Strawman is hoping that you don't catch on to the fact that it is not you who is being billed, and so make the payment as a mistake on your part.

If you don't want to pay this unnecessary charge on behalf of the Strawman, then you can mark the envelope "NO CONTRACT — Return to Sender" and mail it back to the sender. Any subsequent letters can be treated in exactly the same way. As in all cases, do not have any telephone conversations about it, as verbal communications bristle with Legalese verbal traps. At most, say that you wish to deal with any such matters by mail and terminate the call. It does not matter if an employee turns up at your home and hands you a letter or puts it through your mail box. The letter is NOT for you or even addressed to you - it is addressed to the Strawman, so it can be mailed back the same as any other letter.

Recently, Tony Rooke in the UK took a different approach. He refused to pay for a TV licence and went to court over it. There, he stated that he would not pay a TV licence fee because the BBC ("British Broadcasting Corporation") intentionally misrepresented facts about the 9/11 attacks. As is widely known, the BBC reported the collapse of World Trade Centre Building 7 – the 47-story Salomon Brothers' building which was never hit by an airplane but which collapsed at free-fall speed later that day – more than twenty minutes before the collapse occurred.

Rooke stated that the BBC had to have had prior knowledge of that terror attack and so were complicit in the attack. He then showed a recording of the BBC video news broadcast along with considerable additional evidence. The judge agreed that Rooke had a reasonable case to protest and he was found 'not guilty' by the court and was not fined for failure to pay the licensing fee.

If it is still available, the BBC news report of the collapse, showing the building standing behind the reporter, is at

http://tinyurl.com/loulgea

If you wish, you can take a more forceful, direct stance as demonstrated here by a letter issued by Christopher Lees when dealing with a Fixed Penalty Notice charge:

Dear Sirs,

Please read the following notice thoroughly and carefully before responding. It is a notice. It informs you. It means what it says.

The reason why you need to read it carefully is simple. I am offering conditional agreement. This removes controversy, and means that you no longer have any ultimate recourse to a court of law in this matter, because there is no controversy upon which it could adjudicate. You always have the option of dragging these conditions into a court of law only to be told that they are, indeed, lawful. That is, of course,

always your prerogative should you decide to waste your time.

For this reason it is important that you consider and respond to the offer in substance. The "nearest official form" will not suffice, and consequently is likely to be ignored by myself without any dishonor on my part.

On the other hand there is a time-limit on the agreement being offered. It is reasonable, and if it runs out then you and all associated parties are in default, removing any and all lawful excuse on your part for proceeding in this matter.

For these reasons it is recommended that you carefully consider this notice and respond in substance, which means actually addressing the points raised herein.

You have apparently made allegations of criminal conduct against me.

You have apparently made demands upon me.

I do not understand those apparent demands and therefore cannot lawfully fulfil them. I seek clarification of your document so that I may act according to the law and maintain my entire body of inalienable Natural Rights.

Failure to accept this offer to clarify, and to do so completely and in good faith within 7 (seven) days will be deemed by all parties to mean that you and your principal or other parties abandon all demands upon me.

I conditionally accept your offer to agree that I am a legal fiction "person" Mr. Christopher Mark Lees and that I owe £70 for services rendered by your company, upon proof of claim of all of the following:

1. Upon proof of claim that I am a person, and not a human being.

2. Upon proof of claim that you know what a "person" actually is in legal terms.

3. Upon proof of claim that you know the difference

between a "human being" and a "person" legally speaking.

4. Upon proof of claim that you know the difference between the terms "legal" and "lawful".

5. Upon proof of claim that I am legal fiction "person" Mr. Christopher Mark Lees, being the entity to which your paperwork was addressed, and not Christopher of the Lees family, as commonly called.

6. Upon proof of claim that the charge was the result of a lawful investigation unmarred by prejudice.

7. Upon proof of claim that I am a member of the society whose statutes and subsisting regulations you are enforcing.

8. Upon proof of claim that I showed you some sort of identification.

9. Upon proof of claim that there is a nameable society that I belong to and that the laws covered within any alleged transgressions state that they apply to me within that named society.

Sincerely and without ill will, vexation or frivolity,

By: ***_____ *** (Agent)

Christopher of the Lees family

WITHOUT PREJUDICE, i.e. all Natural Inalienable Rights Reserved

Please address all future correspondence in the matter to a direct Human Self, namely Christopher of the Lees family, as commonly called.

Encl: Original paperwork as received.

CONSENT

All men are born equal and so nobody has the right to command you, make demands of you or force you to do anything. The most that anyone can do is to make you an offer to perform.

Even though they may say that it is an "Order", or a "Demand", or a "Summons", it is in reality an offer which you are free to accept or not as you so choose. This is why they keep using "Applications", "Registrations" and "Submissions" as those things give them power over you through your unwitting consent. They are hoping that you will break the law by the way that you deal with their offer. If you just ignore the offer, you are stepping into what is called "dishonor". The only effective way of dealing with the offer is "conditional acceptance" as already mentioned. If you accept their offer without imposing any conditions, then you are accepting that they have the power to order you around, and that places you under their authority, because you have just chosen to accept their offer (even though you may not understand that you are accepting their offer for them to have authority over you).

They also want to get you arguing with them since that also places you in "dishonor", and if there is a court case involved, the judge just looks to see who is in dishonor. Remember, in civil cases the court is a commercial operation where the judge doesn't care who is right or wrong, just who will pay the court. So, we accept all offers but with our conditions attached to each offer, and that prevents them taking us to court - remember, courts only deal with disputes and if you conditionally accept each offer there won't be any dispute and so there can't be any court involvement. Some offers are "Notices" and a notice has to be clear, unequivocal, and concise. You can discharge a Notice by seeking clarification, that is by writing back, asking the meaning of a word, stating that you don't understand the word. They were hoping that you would just ignore the Notice and so go into dishonor and become liable.

A Parking Ticket is a "Notice", and please be aware that a Parking Ticket is not a bill, but instead it is a Notice telling you that there is something to which you should pay attention. So you write back saying that you have noticed their Notice and as they appear to think that you owe them money, you are happy to pay, but first you need some verification before payment is made.

"First, there is a need to verify the debt, so please send me a bill with a human signature on it. Also, I need to see the lawful, two-party contract supporting that bill". As they can't supply either of those things, it kills the claim stone dead, so just keep insisting that they either supply those things or else stop bothering you.

An interesting alternative is that if they send you a final notice marked "Remittance", then that piece of paper actually has the value of the money amount written on it. The really silly thing is that you have the option to write "Accepted for value" on that piece of paper, sign it with your name and the date, and mail it back to them, and technically, that concludes the matter by paying the amount demanded. Who was it that said "it's a mad, mad, mad, mad world"? Actually, the payment comes out of the vast amount of money which your Strawman has accumulated over the years, and your signing the document as "Accepted for value", authorizes them to take the payment from your Strawman account and that suits them as well as yourself. Writing "Accepted for Value" means that you are authorizing them to take the amount they specify out of the Strawman account which has such a large amount in it that the balance will hardly be affected at all.

SOCIETY

We come now to the very difficult subject of American society. I certainly don't know all the answers in this area. A society is a group of people who willingly join together and abide by a set of rules decided on by members of that society. Loosely speaking, the system which has been set up by the commercial companies who have control of the United States, is a society. It is a society which has good features and bad features as well.

Common sense says that there is an advantage for any large number of people to organize themselves together and have skilled specialists provide paid services for the other members of that society.

For example, having a communal collection to enable roads, water supplies, sewerage and the like, certainly makes sense. A National Health Service also looks like a good idea as does having social welfare benefits for those who are unfortunate enough to become ill or who are unable to find work. However, such things have been subverted by those in charge, and manoeuvred into a state where these things serve their ends rather than the needs of the general population.

While a country-wide medical service sounds like a good thing, it has been reported that the price of some of the medicines supplied to the National Health Service now cost literally ten times what they did two years ago. This looks very much as if the people in control of that service are using it to make massive profits on pharmaceuticals, and probably many other services such as parking fees where millions per year are made from people who have no option but to park in the hospital grounds. So, what looks like a sensible arrangement, appears to have been converted to something different. Perhaps this is an unduly cynical view, but it is certainly in line with many of the other scams which are being run.

Income Tax was introduced as a temporary measure in connection with a war (and who organizes wars?). It has never been removed and yet the country did not seem to have any major problems when there was no Income Tax. The employees of the commercial company which runs the country - those people who take the title of Member of Congress or some similar meaningless title, spend a lot of time thinking up "new legislation" which if it can be introduced without too many people noticing it, will   become a "statute". I suggest that the main intention of all legislation is to provide a smoke-screen to hide additional charges which members of the public are required to pay. An argument can be that "you elected" those politicians, so you must abide by whatever they dictate. This carefully avoids mentioning the fact that those politicians have nothing to do with the public, other than giving the appearance that the public has some say in what happens, while the reality is that everything that happens is dictated by the (non-elected) owners of the companies in charge.

The payment of benefits to those in need looks like a very good and necessary thing, but the people in charge see it as an admission that the adult is not capable of taking care of himself and so they literally think of these ordinary people as "cattle" (their word, not mine). What they ignore is the fact that their many, many direct and indirect taxes and charges, along with the low level of pay which they reckon that people can be made to work for, are the things which have many ordinary, hard-working people in the very poor financial positions which they despise. They are willing to cheat, steal and lie while the ordinary person is not comfortable doing those things. So, what should be a good and helpful system, has been changed into an oppressive thing which is used to force people into dependency.

While a certain level of public contribution for what are thought of as being essential services, is understandable and a desirable thing, that the system has been twisted into a mechanism to enslave and defraud ordinary people. It has long since reached a ridiculous level with the average person being expected to pay Income Tax, Council Tax, Inheritance Tax, National Insurance, Capital Gains Tax, Sales tax on house purchases, Value Added Tax, Parking charges, Airport charges, Fuel Tax, Road Tax, Import Duty, Tax on alcohol, Tax on tobacco, payments for a driving licence, passport ... the list goes on and on and on with additional items are added all the time.

People who have been caught for many years in this system will have already paid in so much that they will not want to leave the system and lose the benefits for which they have been paying so long. Others may well consider starting to refuse to pay some of the things demanded of the Strawman. This is a personal choice and one which should be thought about carefully before any action is taken.

Please note that this document does not provide you with legal advice, but instead, presents facts for information purposes only. If you want legal advice, then consult a lawyer.

THE ARMED SERVICES

The commercial company which has chosen the name "The United States, Inc.", has a large number of people employed in what it calls the "United States Armed Services". Most countries have a similar arrangement. If you were asked "what is the purpose of these armed and trained people?" How would you reply?

It may surprise you to know that the people who employ them hire them to protect themselves (the employers) from their enemies.

Not too startling an idea you say. Yes, as you say, not too startling a revelation, but what may surprise you to discover is that the enemy is quite openly stated to be YOU! So, not only do they describe you as a "monster" but also as their "enemy".

Because they are so heavily outnumbered, they are actually frightened of you and feel that they need armed bodyguards and heavy locked doors to keep them safe from the anger of ordinary people, if they every find out how they are being manipulated and robbed. In passing, they consider anybody who asks permission to do something which they are already entitled to do under Common Law, to be a "Child of the State" and so, of no consequence.

Let's check out a possible scenario. You take some young people to a McDonald's restaurant and order several meals. When the food has been prepared, the manager says, "I will make a deal with you: you can have your meals for free if you just take this loaded revolver and go over to that corner table and shoot that man dead. There will be no comeback as I am authorizing you to do it". Having blinked a few times, you ask why you should shoot him dead when he has never done anything to you. The manager then says, "He has never done anything to me neither, but he has a lot of money in his wallet and I want to steal it, so just go and shoot him dead, it's

OK, because I am telling you to do it for me".

Sound a bit mad? Well, it should do so as murder is a criminal offense under Common Law, and somebody telling you to do it, and that it is OK because they say so, is quite ridiculous. Nobody has the authority to tell you to murder somebody - remember, all of us were born with exactly the same privileges and rights, and nobody has authority over anyone else, and most definitely not to be able to authorize murder.

The owners of the commercial company which amusingly we think of as "the government" stand in the same position as the manager of McDonald's, and have the same lack of authority to breach Common Law by sending their armed employees into another country to kill the people there — people who have done them no harm whom they want to rob.

All recessions and wars are deliberately instigated by the people who gain financially from them.

Did you ever wonder why vast sums of "public" money are spent every year on arms? Who owns the companies that make the profits from selling these arms? Who gets the profits from rebuilding the places damaged or destroyed by your very own army? Who makes a profit from "lending" vast sums of imaginary money to a country which has been devastated by their unprovoked actions, creating an imaginary debt which can never be repaid?

Since World War Two, more than four million people have died as a result of commercial companies interfering in other countries, and every one of those deaths was a criminal offense under Common Law. These companies believe that they and their employees are above the law and so they do whatever they want.

From time to time, these companies demand that people be conscripted into their armed forces, without their consent. Do you ever remember being asked if you would consent to such press-gang operations? If you were asked - did you say "Yes"? And if you did, does it make it lawful to force the people who said "No"? Do you ever get the impression that things are done which breach both your personal rights and the demands of Common Law?

Not only does invading other countries and murdering the people there destroy them, but it also has a major negative impact on the people who joined the armed forces, not being aware that their (commercial) employers are the real terrorists of this world. Do you feel that this is a little far-fetched? Well, it was reported on national TV news on 6th September 2010 that ex-Army Chief General Richard Dannatt claimed that "vested interests" rather than "national security" decided military spending on the wars in Afghanistan and Iraq. All major wars are carried out for commercial reasons, although that fact will never be admitted publicly.

Michael Rivero has put together a concise statement on the situation in America, (which impacts upon the whole world). His statement is at this web location **http://tinyurl.com/b4ah7tt** here he says:

I know that many people have a great deal of difficulty with understanding just how many wars are started for no other purpose than to force private central banks onto nations, so let me share a few examples, in order that you can understand why the US Government is engaged in so many wars against so many foreign nations. There is ample precedent for this.

The United States fought the war of the American Revolution primarily over the Currency Act of King George III, which forced the colonists to conduct their business only with printed bank notes borrowed from the Bank of England at interest. After the Revolution, the new United States adopted a radically different economic system in which the government issued its own value-based money, so that private banks like the Bank of England were not siphoning off the wealth of the people through interest-bearing bank notes.

"The refusal of King George III to allow the colonies to operate an honest money system, which freed the ordinary man from the clutches of the money manipulators, was probably the prime cause of the revolution". -- Benjamin Franklin, Founding Father.

But bankers are nothing if not dedicated to their schemes to acquire your wealth, and they know how easy it is to corrupt the leaders of a nation. Just one year after Mayer Amschel Rothschild had uttered his infamous statement: *"Let me issue and control a nation's money and I care not who makes the laws"*, the bankers succeeded in setting up a new Private Central Bank called the First Bank of the United States, largely through the efforts of the Rothschild's chief US supporter, Alexander Hamilton.

Founded in 1791, by the end of its twenty year charter the First Bank of the United States had almost ruined the nation's economy, while enriching the bankers. Congress refused to renew the charter signaling their intention to go back to a state-issued value-based currency, on which the people paid no interest at all to any banker. This resulted in a threat from Nathan Mayer Rothschild against the US Government: *"Either the application for renewal of the charter is granted, or the United States will find itself involved in a most disastrous war".* Congress still refused to renew the   charter for the First Bank of the United States, whereupon Nathan Mayer Rothschild railed, *"Teach those impudent Americans a lesson! Bring them back to Colonial status!"*

Financed by the Rothschild-controlled Bank of England, Britain then launched the war of 1812 to re-colonize the United States and force it back into slavery to the Bank of England, or to plunge it into so much debt that the people would be forced to accept a new private central bank. The plan worked. Even though the War of 1812 *appeared* to be won by the United States, Congress was forced to grant a new charter for yet another private bank issuing the public currency as loans at interest, and that was the Second Bank of the United States. Once again, private bankers were in control of the nation's money supply and cared not who made the laws or how many British and American soldiers had to die for it.

Once again the nation was plunged into debt, unemployment, and poverty through the plundering of the private central bank, and in 1832 Andrew Jackson successfully campaigned for his second term as President under the slogan, "Jackson And No Bank!" True to his word, Jackson succeeded in blocking the renewal of the charter for the Second Bank of the United States.

"Gentlemen! I too have been a close observer of the doings of the Bank of the United States. I have had men watching you for a long time, and am convinced that you have used the funds of the bank to speculate in the breadstuffs of the country. When you won, you divided the profits amongst yourselves, and when you lost, you charged it to the bank. You tell me that if I take the deposits from the bank and annul its charter I shall ruin ten thousand families. That may be true, gentlemen, but that is Your sin! If I let you go on, you will ruin fifty thousand families, and that would be My sin! You are a den of vipers and thieves. I have determined to rout you out, and by the Eternal, God, (bringing his fist down on the table) *I will rout you out!"*

— Andrew Jackson, shortly before ending the charter of the Second Bank of the United States. [From the original minutes of the Philadelphia committee of citizens sent to meet with President Jackson (February 1834), according to *Andrew Jackson and the Bank of the United States* (1928) by Stan V. Henkel].

Shortly after President Jackson (the only American President to actually pay off the National Debt) ended the Second Bank of the United States, there was an attempted assassination which failed when both pistols used by the assassin, Richard Lawrence, failed to fire. Lawrence later said that *"with Jackson dead, money would be more plentyful"*.

Of course, the present day American public school system is as subservient to the bankers' wishes to keep certain items of history from you, just as the corporate media is subservient to Monsanto's wishes to keep the dangers of Genetically Modified foodstuffs from you, and the Global Warming cult's wishes to conceal from you the fact that the Earth has actually been cooling for the last 16 years. Thus is should come as little surprise, that much of the real reasons for the events of the Civil War are not well known to the average American.

When the Confederacy constitutionally seceded from the United States, the bankers once again saw the opportunity for a rich harvest of debt, and offered to fund Lincoln's efforts to bring the south back into the union by force, but at 30% interest. Lincoln remarked that he would not free the black man by enslaving the white man to the bankers, so using his authority as President, he issued a new government currency, the "greenback".

This was a direct threat to the wealth and power of the central bankers of the United States, who responded quickly.

"If this mischievous financial policy, which has its origin in North America, becomes entrenched, then that Government will issue it's own money without cost. It will pay off debts and be without debt. It will have all the money necessary to carry on its commerce. It will become prosperous to a degree which is without precedent in the history of the world. The brains, and wealth of all countries will migrate to North America. That country must be destroyed or it will destroy every monarchy on the globe".

— The London Times responding to Lincoln's decision to issue government greenbacks to finance the Civil War, rather than agree to private banker's loans at 30% interest.

In 1872 New York bankers sent a letter to every bank in the United States, urging them to fund any newspapers which opposed government-issued money (Lincoln's greenbacks):

"Dear Sir: It is advisable to do all in your power to sustain such prominent daily and weekly newspapers... as will oppose the issuing of greenback paper money, and that you also with-hold patronage or favors from all applicants who are not will-ing to oppose the Government issue of money. Let the Government issue the coin and the banks issue the paper money of the country. To restore to circulation the Government issue of money, will be to provide the people with money, and will therefore seriously affect your individual profit as bankers and lenders".
— "Triumphant plutocracy"; the story of American public life from 1870 to 1920, by Lynn Wheeler.

"It will not do to allow the greenback, as it is called, to circulate as money any length of time, as we cannot control that". — ibid.

"Slavery is likely to be abolished by the war, power, and chattel slavery destroyed. This, I and my European friends are in favor of, for slavery is but the owning of labor and carries with it the care for the laborer, while the European plan, led on by England, is for capital to control labor by controlling the wages. THIS CAN BE DONE BY CONTROLLING THE MONEY"! — ibid.

Goaded by the private bankers, much of Europe supported the Confederacy against the Union, with the expectation that victory over Lincoln would mean the end of the Greenback. France and Britain considered an outright attack on the United States to aid the confederacy, but were held at bay by Russia, which had just ended the serfdom system and had a state central bank similar to the system the United States had been founded on. Left free of European intervention, the Union won the war, and Lincoln announced his intention to go on issuing greenbacks. Following Lincoln's assassination, the greenbacks were pulled from circulation and the American people forced to go back to an economy based on bank notes borrowed at interest from the private bankers.

Finally, in 1913, the Private Central Bankers of Europe, in particular the Rothschilds of Great Britain and the Warburgs of Germany, met with their American financial collaborators on Jekyll Island, Georgia to form a new banking cartel with the express purpose of forming the Third Bank of the United States, with the aim of placing complete control of the United States money supply once again under the control of private bankers. Owing to hostility over the previous banks, the name was changed to "The Federal Reserve" system in order to grant the new bank a quasi-governmental image, but in fact it is a privately owned bank, no more "Federal" than Federal Express. Indeed, in 2012, the Federal Reserve successfully rebuffed a Freedom of Information Lawsuit by Bloomberg News on the grounds that as a private banking corporation and not actually a part of the government, the Freedom of Information Act did not apply to the operations of the Federal Reserve. The year 1913 proved to be a transformative year for the nation's economy, first with the passage of the 16th "income tax" Amendment and the false claim that it had been ratified.

"I think that if you were to go back and try top find and review the ratification of the 16th Amendment, which was the internal revenue, the income tax, I think that if you went back and examined that carefully, you would find that a sufficient number of States never ratified that Amendment". — U.S. District Court Judge James C. Fox (Sullivan v United States, 2003).

Later in 1913, apparently unwilling to risk another questionable amendment, Congress passed the Federal Reserve Act over the Christmas holiday, while members of Congress who were opposed to the measure were at home. This was a very underhanded deal, as the Constitution which explicitly grants Congress the authority to issue the public currency, does not authorize it to delegate that authority to another party, and so it should have required a new Amendment to allow Congress to transfer that authority to a private bank. But Congress passed it, and President Woodrow Wilson signed it (as he had promised the bankers that he would, in exchange for generous campaign contributions). Wilson later regretted that decision, stating in 1919:

"I am a most unhappy man. I have unwittingly ruined my country. A great industrial nation is now controlled by its system of credit. We are no longer a government by free opinion, no longer a government by conviction and vote of the majority, but a government by the opinion and duress of a small group of dominant men".

The very next year, World War I started, and it is important to remember that prior to the creation of the Federal Reserve, there was no such thing as a world war. No profits — No wars.

The First World War started between Austria-Hungary and Serbia, but quickly shifted to focus to Germany, whose industrial capacity was seen as an economic threat to Great Britain, who saw the decline of the British Pound as a result of too much emphasis on financial activity to the neglect of agriculture, industrial development, and infrastructure (not unlike the present day United States).

Although pre-war Germany had a private central bank, that bank was heavily restricted, and inflation kept to reasonable levels. Under government control, investment was guaranteed to internal economic development, and Germany was seen as a major power. So, in the media of the day, Germany was portrayed as the prime instigator of World War One, and subsequently, not just defeated, but had its industrial base flattened.

Following the Treaty of Versailles (June, 1919) Germany was ordered to pay the war costs of all of the participating nations, even though Germany had not actually started the war. This amounted to three times the value of all of Germany itself. Germany's private central bank, to which Germany had gone deeply into debt to pay the costs of the war, broke free of government control, and massive inflation followed (mostly triggered by currency speculators) permanently trapping the German people in endless debt.

When the Weimar Republic economically collapsed, it opened the door for the National Socialists to take power. Their first financial move was to issue their own state currency which was not borrowed from private central banks. Freed from having to pay interest on the money in circulation, Germany blossomed and quickly began to rebuild its industry. The media called it "The German Miracle". TIME magazine lionized Hitler for the amazing improvement in life for the German people, and the explosion of German industry, and even named him TIME Magazine's "Man Of The Year", in 1938.

Once again, Germany's industrial output became a threat to Great Britain, resulting in these comments:

"Should Germany merchandise (do business) *again in the next 50 years, we have led this war* (WWI) *in vain".* — Winston Churchill in The Times (1919)

"We will force this war upon Hitler, if he wants it or not". — Winston Churchill (1936 broadcast)

"Germany becomes too powerful. We have to crush it." — Winston Churchill (November 1936 speaking to US - General Robert E. Wood).

"This war is an English war and its goal is the destruction of Germany". — Winston Churchill (- Autumn 1939 broadcast).

Germany's **state-issued** **value-based currency** was also a direct threat to the wealth and power of the private central banks, and as early as 1933 they started to organize a global boycott against Germany to strangle this upstart ruler who thought he could break free of private central banks!

As had been the case in World War I, Great Britain and other nations threatened by Germany's economic power looked for an excuse to go to war, and as public anger in Germany grew over the boycott, Hitler foolishly gave them that excuse. Years later, in a spirit of candor, the real reasons for that war were made clear:

"The war wasn't only about abolishing fascism, but to conquer sales markets. We could have, if we had intended to, prevented this war from breaking out without firing one shot, but we didn't want to". — Winston Churchill to Truman (Fultun, USA March 1946).

"Germany's unforgivable crime before WWII was its attempt to loosen its economy out of the world trade system and to build up an independent exchange system from which world-finance couldn't profit any more. ... We butchered the wrong pig". — Winston Churchill (The Second World War - Bern, 1960).

As a side note, we need to step back before WWII and recall Marine Major General Smedley Butler. In 1933, Wall Street bankers and financiers had bankrolled the successful coups by both Hitler and Mussolini. Brown Brothers Harriman in New York was financing Hitler right up to the day war was declared with Germany. And they decided that a fascist dictatorship in the United States, based on the one in Italy, would be far better for their business interests than Roosevelt's "New Deal" which threatened massive wealth re-distribution to recapitalize the working and middle class of America. So the Wall Street tycoons recruited General Butler to lead the overthrow of the US Government and install a "Secretary of General Affairs" who would be answerable to Wall Street and not to the people, and would crush social unrest and shut down all labor unions.

General Butler pretended to go along with the scheme but then exposed the plot to Congress. Congress, then as now in the pocket of the Wall Street bankers, refused to act. When Roosevelt learned of the planned coup, he demanded the arrest of the plotters, but the plotters simply reminded Roosevelt that if any one of them were sent to prison, their friends on Wall Street would deliberately collapse the still-fragile economy and blame Roosevelt for it. Roosevelt was thus unable to act until the start of WWII, at which time he prosecuted many of the plotters under the "Trading With The Enemy Act".

The Congressional minutes into the coup were finally released in 1967 and became the inspiration for the movie, "Seven Days in May" but with the true financial villains erased from the script.

"I spent 33 years and four months in active military service as a member of our country's most agile military force -- the Marine Corps. I served in all commissioned ranks from second lieutenant to Major General. During that period I spent more of my time being a high-class muscle man for Big Business, for Wall Street, and for the bankers. In short, I was a racketeer, a gangster for capitalism. I suspected that I was just a part of a racket at the time. Now I am sure of it. Like all members of the military profession I never had an original thought until I left the service. My mental faculties remained in suspended animation, while I obeyed the orders of the higher-ups. This is typical with everyone in the military service. Thus I helped make Mexico, and especially Tampico, safe for American oil interests in 1914. I helped make Haiti and Cuba a decent place for the National City Bank boys to collect revenues in. I helped in the raping of half a dozen Central American republics for the benefit of Wall Street. The record of racketeering is long. I helped purify Nicaragua for the

international banking house of Brown Brothers in 1909-12. I brought light to the Dominican Republic for American sugar interests in 1916. In China in 1927 I helped see to it that Standard Oil went on its way unmolested. During those years, I had, as the boys in the back room would say, a swell racket. I was rewarded with honors, medals and promotion. Looking back on it, I feel I might have given Al Capone a few hints. The best he could do was to operate his racket in three city districts. I operated on three continents". — General Smedley Butler, former US Marine Corps Commandant, 1935.

As President, John F. Kennedy understood the predatory nature of private central banking, he understood why Andrew Jackson fought so hard to end the Second Bank of the United States. So Kennedy wrote and signed Executive Order 11110 which ordered the US Treasury to issue a new public currency, the United States Note.

Kennedy's United States Notes were not borrowed from the Federal Reserve but created by the US Government and backed by the silver stockpiles held by the US Government. It represented a return to the system of economics on which the United States had been founded, and this was perfectly legal for Kennedy to do. All told, some four and a half billion dollars went into public circulation, eroding interest payments to the Federal Reserve and loosening their control over the nation. Five months later John F. Kennedy was assassinated in Dallas Texas, and the United States Notes, pulled from circulation and destroyed (except for samples held by collectors). John J. McCloy, President of the Chase Manhattan Bank, and President of the World Bank, was named as part of the Warren Commission, presumably to make certain that the banking dimensions behind the assassination were concealed from the public.

As we enter the twelfth year of what future history will most certainly describe as World War III, we need to examine the financial dimensions behind the wars.

Towards the end of World War II, when it became obvious that the allies were going to win and dictate the post war environment, the major world economic powers met at Bretton Woods, a luxury resort in New Hampshire, in July 1944, and hammered out the Bretton Woods agreement for international finance. The British Pound lost its position as the global trade and reserve currency and its place was taken by the US dollar (part of the price demanded by Roosevelt in exchange for the US entry into the war). Without the economic advantages of being the world's central currency, Britain was forced to nationalize the Bank of England in 1946. The Bretton Woods agreement was ratified in 1945, and in addition to making the US dollar the global reserve and trade currency, obliged the signatory nations to tie their currencies to the dollar. The nations which ratified Bretton Woods did so on two conditions. The first was that the Federal Reserve would refrain from over-printing the dollar as a means to loot real products and produce from other nations in exchange for ink and paper; basically an imperial tax. That assurance was backed up by the second, which was that the US dollar would always be convertible to gold at $35 per ounce.

Of course, the Federal Reserve, being a private bank and not answerable to the US Government, did start overprinting paper dollars, and much of the perceived prosperity of the 1950s and 1960s was the result of foreign nations' obligations to accept the paper notes as being worth gold at the rate of $35 an ounce.

Then in 1970, France looked at the huge pile of paper notes sitting in their vaults, for which real French products like wine and cheese had been traded, and notified the United States government that they would exercise their option under Bretton Woods to return the paper notes for gold at the $35 per ounce exchange rate. Of course, the United States had nowhere near the gold to redeem the paper notes, so on August 15th, 1971, Richard Nixon "temporarily" suspended the gold convertibility of the US Federal Reserve Notes.

This "Nixon Shock" effectively ended Bretton Woods and many global currencies started to disengage from the US dollar. Worse still, since the United States had collateralized their loans with the nation's gold reserves, it quickly became apparent that the US Government did not in fact have enough gold to cover its outstanding debts. Foreign nations began to get nervous about their loans to the US and understandably were reluctant to lend any additional money to the United States without some form of collateral. So Richard Nixon started the environmental movement, with the EPA and its various programs such as "wilderness zones", "Road-less areas", "Heritage rivers", "Wetlands", all of which took vast areas of public lands and made them off limits to the American people who were technically the owners of those lands. But Nixon had little concern for the environment, for the real purpose of this land grab under the guise of the environment was to pledge those pristine lands and their vast mineral resources as collateral on the national debt. The plethora of different programs was simply to conceal the true scale of how much American land was being pledged to foreign lenders as collateral on the government's debts; eventually almost 25% of the nation itself.

With open lands for collateral already in short supply, the US Government embarked on a new program to shore up sagging international demand for the dollar. The United States approached the world's oil producing nations, mostly in the Middle East, and offered them a deal. In exchange for only selling their oil for dollars, the United States would guarantee the military safety of those oil-rich nations. The oil rich nations would agree to spend and invest their US paper dollars inside the United States, in particular in US Treasury Bonds, redeemable through future generations of US taxpayers. The concept was labelled the "petrodollar". In effect, the US, no longer able to back the dollar with gold, was now backing it with oil. Other peoples' oil, and the necessity to control those oil nations in order to prop up the dollar has shaped America's foreign policy in the region ever since.

But as America's manufacturing and agriculture has declined, the oil producing nations faced a dilemma. Those piles of US Federal Reserve notes were not able to purchase much from the United States because the United States had little (other than real estate) which anyone wanted to buy.

Europe's cars and aircraft were superior and less costly, while experiments with GMO food crops led to nations refusing to buy

US food exports. Israel's constant belligerence against its neighbors caused them to wonder if the US could actually keep up their end of the petrodollar arrangement. Oil-producing nations started to talk of selling their oil for whatever currency the purchasers chose to use. Iraq, already hostile to the United States, following Desert Storm, demanded the right to sell their oil for Euros, in 2000, and the United Nations agreed to allow it in 2002 under the Oil for Food program instituted following Desert Storm. One year later the United States re-invaded Iraq, lynched Saddam Hussein, and placed Iraq's oil back on the world market only for US dollars.

Following 9-11, the US policy shift away from being an impartial broker of peace in the Middle East to one of unquestioned support for Israel's aggressions, only further eroded confidence in the Petrodollar deal and even more oil-producing nations started openly talking of oil trade for other global currencies.

Over in Libya, Muammar Gaddafi had instituted a state-owned central bank and a value-based trade currency, the Gold Dinar. Gaddafi announced that Libya's oil was for sale, but only for the gold Dinar. Other African nations, seeing the rise of the Gold Dinar and the Euro, even as the US dollar continued its inflation-driven decline, flocked to the new Libyan currency for trade. This move had the potential to seriously undermine the global hegemony of the dollar. French President Nicolas Sarkozy reportedly went so far as to call Libya a "threat" to the financial security of the world.

So, the United States invaded Libya, brutally murdered Gaddafi (the object lesson of Saddam's lynching not being enough of a message, apparently), imposed a private central bank, and returned Libya's oil output to dollars only. The gold that was to have been made into the Gold Dinars is, as of last report, unaccounted for.

According to General Wesley Clark, the master plan for the "dollarification" of the world's oil nations included seven targets, Iraq; Syria; Lebanon; Libya; Somalia; Sudan; and Iran (Venezuela —which dared to sell their oil to China for the Yuan—is a late 8th addition). What is notable about the original seven nations originally targeted by the US is that none of them are members of the Bank for International Settlements, the private central bankers private central bank, located in Switzerland. This meant that these nations were deciding for themselves how to run their nations' economies, rather than submit to the private international banks.

Now the banker's gun sights are on Iran, which dares to have a government controlled central bank and sell their oil for whatever currency they choose. The war agenda is, as always, to force Iran's oil to be sold only for dollars and to force them to accept a privately owned central bank.

The German government just recently asked for the return of some of their gold bullion from the Bank of France and the New York Federal Reserve. France has said it will take 5 years to return Germany's gold. The United States has said they will need 8 years to return Germany's gold. This suggests strongly that the Bank of France and the NY Federal Reserve have used the deposited gold for other purposes, and they are scrambling to find new gold to cover the shortfall and prevent a gold run. So France suddenly invades Mali, ostensibly to combat Al Qaeda, with the US joining in.

Mali just happens to be one of the world's largest gold producers with gold accounting for 80% of Mali exports. War for the bankers does not get more obvious than that!

Americans have been raised by a public school system and media that constantly assures them that the reasons for all these wars and assassinations are many and varied. The US claims to bring democracy to the conquered lands (they haven't). The usual result of a US overthrow is the imposition of a dictatorship—such as the 1953 CIA overthrow of Iran's democratically elected government of Mohammad Mosaddegh and the imposition of the Shah—or the 1973 CIA overthrow of Chile's democratically elected government of President Salvador Allende, and the imposition of Agusto Pinochet)—or to save a people from a cruel oppressor, revenge for 9-11; or that tired worn-out catch all excuse for invasion: "weapons of mass destruction". Assassinations are always passed off as "crazed lone nuts" to obscure the real agenda.

The real agenda is simple. It is enslavement of the people by the creation of a false sense of obligation. That obligation is false because the private Central Banking system, by design, always creates more debt than money with which to repay that debt. Private Central Banking is not Science, it is a Religion; a set of arbitrary rules created to benefit the Priesthood, meaning the owners of the Private Central Bank.

The fraud persists, with often lethal results, because the people are tricked into believing that this is the way life is supposed to be and no alternative exists or should be dreamed of. The same was true of two earlier systems of enslavement, Rule by Divine Right and Slavery, both of which are systems designed to trick people into obedience, and both of which are now recognized by modern civilization as illegitimate. Now we are entering a time in human history where we will recognize that "rule by debt", or rule by private Central Bankers issuing the public currency as a loan at interest, is equally illegitimate.

It only works as long as people allow themselves to believe that this is the way life is supposed to be.

But understand this above all else, private Central Banks do not exist to serve the people, the community, or the nation. Private Central Banks exist to serve their owners, to make them rich beyond the dreams of Midas and all for the cost of paper, ink, and the right bribe to the right official.

Behind all these wars, all these assassinations, the hundred million horrible deaths from all the wars lies a single policy of dictatorship. The private central bankers allow rulers to rule only on the condition that the people of a nation remain enslaved to the private central banks. Failing that, any ruler will be killed, and their nation invaded by those other nations which are already enslaved to private central banks.

The so-called "clash of civilizations" we read about on the corporate media is really a war between banking systems, with the private central bankers forcing themselves on to the rest of the world, no matter how many millions must die for it. Indeed the constant hatemongering against Muslims lies in a simple fact. Like the ancient Christians (prior to the Knights Templar's private banking system) Muslims forbid usury (the lending of money at interest), and that is the reason why the American government and media insist that Muslims must be converted or killed. They refuse to submit to currencies issued at interest. They refuse to be debt slaves. So off to war American children must go, to spill their blood for the gold of the money-junkies. We barely survived the last two world wars. In the nuclear/bio-weapon age, are the private central bankers willing to risk incinerating the whole planet just to feed their greed? Apparently so.

Flag waving and propaganda aside, all modern wars are wars by and for the private bankers, fought and bled for by third parties unaware of the true reason why they are expected to be crippled and killed. The process is quite simple. As soon as the Private Central Bank issues its currency as a loan at interest, the public is forced deeper and deeper into debt. When the people are reluctant to borrow any more, that is when the Keynesian economists demand the government borrow more to keep the pyramid scheme working. When both the people and government refuse to borrow any more, that is when the wars start, to plunge everyone even deeper into debt to pay for the war, then after the war to borrow more to rebuild. When the war is over, the people have about the same as they did before the war, except the graveyards are far larger and everyone is in debt to the private bankers for the next century. This is why Brown Brothers Harriman in New York funded the rise of Adolf Hitler.

As long as Private Central Banks are allowed to exist, inevitably — as night follows day — there will be poverty, hopelessness, and millions of deaths in endless World Wars, until the Earth itself is sacrificed to Mammon in flames. The path to true peace on Earth lies in the abolishment of all private central banking everywhere, and a return to the state-issued value-based currencies that allow nations and people to become prosperous.

SUMMARY

Before you were born, the bankers operated a scam intended to rob all members of the general public. They removed all forms of money and replaced it with worthless notes which read "I promise to pay the bearer"... (with another worthless bank note). They then managed to do away with the government and replace it with a group of commercial companies which they own. They cunningly named these companies so that they look like a government. They took over the printing of the worthless bank notes with their private company called "The Bank of England" which is meant to sound like a government organization (although it most definitely isn't).

The next step in their cunning plan, was to get their company which sounds like the government, to ask their other company "The [non-federal] Federal Reserve" to print them lots of (worthless) money and to charge interest on that money, over and above the face "value" of the currency. This excess interest amount is called the "National Debt" in order to fool ordinary people into believing that their country somehow owes somebody large amounts of money. Firstly, there is actually nothing owed at all. Secondly, there is no money. Thirdly, the country does not owe anything, and in the unlikely event that there were a genuine debt, then it has nothing to do with ordinary people as it is just a national debt incurred by one commercial company to another commercial company (owned by the same people). This supposed debt has been boosted over the years to a ridiculous level which could never, ever be paid off, and you will no doubt be glad to learn that all income tax is now paid to the owners of these commercial companies. Isn't it great to be paying vast sums of money to a commercial company which has never done anything for you and which holds you in utter contempt because you haven't discovered their scam and continue to pay lots of ridiculous taxes, fees and charges, none of which you need to pay at all. Combined, these charges amount to more than 80% of a person's earned income - do you enjoy living on one fifth of what you actually earn?

To strengthen their scam, they have invented a language of lies called "legal terminology" where they have changed the meanings of ordinary English words in order to abuse and rob ordinary members of the public. They have set up a company called "The Law Society" to train up unscrupulous people in their methods of deception and lies. Their commercial company which pretends to be the government, keeps inventing new "statutes" which they pretend are laws (which they most definitely are not) and they keep telling everybody that they "must obey these laws", and they have subverted policeman and policewomen and convinced them that they have to enforce these statutes. The primary aim of these statutes is to take cash, goods and property from members of the public who have not yet discovered that it is a scam being run against them. Many police officers are probably themselves ignorant of the fact that statutes are purely optional and no human is actually bound by them.

Just to clarify the situation, breaches of The Law are dealt with in a genuine court with a jury. All other matters, such as taxation, bank loans, parking restrictions, speed limits, and the like, are dealt with in a fake "court" which is a commercial company and part of a violent protection racket style scam which is wholly unlawful, but enforced by violence, threats and intimidation using bailiffs and police to protect the bailiffs from being attacked. There has never been any law which demands that you pay any form of tax, licence or other charge.

What you decide to do is entirely up to yourself. You can continue to give away most of your income to fund people who want to harm you, or you can decide to step outside this corrupt system, and stop paying these people. All humans are born equal, so nobody has the right to order you around, unless you agree to give them that right, and the choice is yours.

AN OVERVIEW OF A POLITICAL CON JOB

If this has all been a lot of new information for you, then it might be useful to have a "thumbnail" sketch of the outrageous confidence trick which is being played on you. So, here it is for your local area, and the same situation is found in almost every other area as well.

It all started before most people were born. It started with two brothers deciding to run a scam which would make them the richest people in the world and rig things so that everybody else worked for them without being aware of that fact. Even though they are literally brothers, in order to distinguish between them we will call them Mr. Government and Mr. Banker because that is what they needed to become in order to run this scam.

Mr. Government set up a very clever system of interlocking commercial companies, choosing names for them which made them look like official government bodies, while in reality, they are just ordinary companies like any high-street shop. In order to strengthen the illusion, Mr. Government hires people to work for him and gives them names like "Congressman" or "Member of Parliament" or some other meaningless working title. He employs most of them to sit around and argue with each other, and from time to time, he swaps them around by asking members of the public to vote for who will be his employees for the next few years.

This is actually very clever, because it makes members of the public believe that their voting makes a difference, while Mr. Government knows that it doesn't as he sets company policy, and he makes all of the decisions, and he really couldn't care less who happen to be his employees at any given moment in time.

Meanwhile, his brother Mr. Banker has set up two commercial companies of his own.

One he calls "The Federal Reserve" or the "Bank of England"

or some other suitable name for his particular location (and yes, there are actually more than two brothers in this family). The other company, he calls "The Mint". He owns both and so decides exactly what each will do.

The action starts and Mr. Government needs money with which to pay his employees, so he asks his brother Mr. Banker to provide some. This is where the fun part starts. Our trusty Mr. Banker "invents" the money and pretends that he has plenty although he actually has none. He "lends" a large amount, say, $1,000,000 to his brother Mr. Government. This costs him nothing as it doesn't even exist, and it is just the first step in the scam.

His brother Mr. Government now says that he has a "National Debt" of $1,200,000 which will increase by 20% (one fifth) every year if it is not paid off completely. His cunning plan of calling it a "National Debt" makes people think that "their country" owes somebody something. The reality is that nobody owes anybody anything. Good, isn't it? Very clever ! Without using anything of any value, the brothers have persuaded people that (a) they have a government (which they don't), and (b) that their country has borrowed money for essential services so their country is in debt to some kindly lender (which it isn't). Very slick — these brothers aren't stupid !

Next, Mr. Government "pays" members of his staff with pieces of paper called "checks" and he sends them to his brother Mr. Banker, to get those pieces of paper exchanged for "money". But, Mr. Banker does not have any money, so instead, he gets his company "The Mint" to print other pieces of paper called "currency" and he passes these out in exchange for his brother's checks, swapping pieces of paper for other pieces of paper.

What is the value of these pieces of paper? The cost of the printing, paper, ink.

At this point, what have the brothers gained? Well, they have got a large number of people working for them, doing whatever they say, and it is costing them nothing.

But, that is just the first step. Now, Mr. Government takes back 80% of what he "paid" to his employees, in the form of taxation. After all, the country is in debt and so Mr. Government has to take money from everybody in order to repay the country's debt – hasn't he? Why does everybody have to pay? Because his employees say so. They invent "statutes" and all kinds of charges designed to move money from ordinary people into the pockets of Mr. Government, who promptly pays most of it to his brother Mr. Banker as the repayment of borrowing (nothing) and interest on the amount borrowed.

Where does the tax money paid by ordinary people come from? It is paid to them to compensate them for the time and effort which they put in when working. This is real money, backed by the goods and services provided by the people who do the work.

This is something of real value, and yet 80% of those valuable assets are taken back from them by Mr. Government. Why do people let this happen? Because they think that they have no choice and will be put in prison if they don't. What they do not understand is that paying tax is optional and they don't have to if they don't want to. Mr. Banker is doing very well out of this. His brother is paying him lots of real money in exchange for the fake money which he invented. So, he decides to expand his business and do exactly the same thing to as many people as he can.

He offers to lend people money (which he will 'invent' and conjure up out of nothing) in order to allow them to buy whatever they want. We will skip the Strawman here and just focus on the actual transaction offered by Mr. Banker.

A house purchaser comes to Mr. Banker, looking for a loan of $100,000. This is a deal on which Mr. Banker can't lose no matter what happens, so he will approve the deal unless he has some very, very good reason for not doing so. After all, it's not going to cost him anything and he will be paid with real money gained through real work done by real people. The deal is for 17% interest per year for 25 years. If the deal runs for the full 25 years, then the borrower may well pay back as much as $433,557 according to a professional mortgage calculator result. That is, you pay back four times what you borrowed, even though what you were given was fake money and what you pay back is real labor-backed money.

But, as Mr Government takes 80% of what you earn before you get to pay the mortgage, you need to earn $2,167,785 in that 25 year period as Mr Government will take $1,734,228 of it away from you in direct and hidden taxes. And to add insult to injury, Mr Government will take a large chunk of that $1,734,228 and give it to his brother Mr Banker in supposed payment of the (fake) "National Debt". So, the house purchaser pays several times the borrowed amount, using his real money.

It gets worse. Mr Banker and Mr Government make sure that not enough currency is issued for people to be physically capable of paying the interest on their loans as there just isn't enough currency in the entire economy for that to be possible. This is another cunning ploy. The people who earn most will not have a problem, but most of the people will have great difficulty and will have very little left after paying their mortgage. The slightest financial problem, such as losing a job, can put the average person in a position where he can't pay the amount demanded. When that happens, and it HAS to happen in a substantial number of cases, then Mr Banker tries to take the property, using some of his brother's "statutes" (which are NOT law) to justify his theft. He may even manage to send in bailiffs ahead of seizing the property, and seize many of the house purchaser's personal possessions as well.

What the house purchaser needs to remember is that the original "loan" was fake and that Mr. Banker never put up anything of value, the purchaser was never told the real amount which he would have to repay, a genuine contract was never drawn up, and in reality, it is not the human borrower which is being asked for the repayment.

Want to know what Mr Banker thinks of any borrower?

**For evil to triumph, all that is necessary
is for good men to do nothing.
— For Example —**

Why did the United States attack Libya, Iraq, Afghanistan and Yemen? Why are US operatives helping to de-stabilize Syria? And why is the United States government so intent in taking down Iran, in spite of the fact that Iran has not attacked any country since 1798?

And, what's next? What are we headed for? When you look at the current trajectory that we are on, it doesn't make any sense at all if you evaluate it on what we are taught in school. And it doesn't make any sense if you base your world view on the propaganda that the mainstream media tries to pass off as news. But it makes perfect sense once you know the real motives of the powers that be. In order to understand those motives, we first have to take a look at history:

In 1945, Britain, with agreement, established the dollar as the world's Reserve Currency, which meant that international commodities were priced in dollars. The agreement, which gave the United States a distinct financial advantage was made under the condition that those dollars would remain redeemable for gold at a consistent rate of $35 per ounce.

The United States promised not to print very much money but this was on the honor system because the Federal reserve refused to allow any audit or supervision of its printing presses.

In the years leading up to 1970, expenditures in the Vietnam War made it clear to many countries that the US was printing far more money than it had in gold, and in response, they began to ask for their gold back. This, of course, set off a rapid decline in the value of the dollar. The situation climaxed in 1971, when France attempted to withdraw it's gold and Nixon refused. On 15th of August, Nixon made the following announcement:

"I have directed the Secretary of the Treasury to take the action necessary to defend the dollar against the speculators. I directed Secretary Connolly to suspend temporarily, the convertibility of the dollar into gold or other reserve assets except in amounts and in conditions determined to be in the interests of monetary stability and in the best interests of the Unites States".

This was obviously not a temporary suspension as he claimed, but rather a permanent default, and for the rest of the world who had entrusted the United States with their gold, it was outright theft. In 1973, President Nixon asked King Faisal of Saudi Arabia to accept only US dollars in payment for oil, and to invest any excess profits in US Treasury Bonds, Notes and Bills. In return, Nixon offered military protection for Saudi oil fields. The same offer was extended to each of the key oil-producing countries, and by 1975, every member of OPEC had agreed to only sell their oil in US dollars.

The act of moving the dollar off gold and tying it to foreign oil, instantly forced every oil-importing country in the world to maintain a constant supply of Federal Reserve paper, and in order to get that paper, they would have to send real physical goods to America. This, was the birth of the Petro Dollar. Paper went out, everything America needed came in, and the United States got very, very rich as a result. It was the largest financial con in recorded history.

The Arms Race of the Cold War was a game of poker. Miliary Expenditures were the chips, and the US had an endless supply of chips. With the Petro Dollar under its belt, it was able to raise the stakes higher and higher, outspending every other country on the planet, until eventually, US military expenditure surpassed that of all of the other nations in the world combined – the Soviet Union never had a chance.

The collapse of the communist bloc in 1991, removed the last counterbalance to American military might. The United States was now an undisputed Super-power with no rival. Many hoped that this would mark the start of a new era of stability and peace. Unfortunately, there were those in high places who had other ideas.

Within that same year, the US invaded Iraq in the first Gulf War, and after crushing the Iraqi military, and destroying their infrastructure, including hospitals and water-purification plants, crippling sanctions were imposed which prevented Iraq's infrastructure from being rebuilt.

Theses sanctions which were initiated by Bush Senior, and sustained throughout the entire Clinton administration, lasted for over a decade and were estimated to have killed more than five hundred thousand children. The Clinton administration was fully aware of these figures.

A TV interviewer speaking to Madeleine Albright, Secretary of State for Clinton, asked: *"We have heard that half a million children have died, I mean, that's more children that died than in Hiroshima, and is the price worth it?"*

To which Madeleine Albright replied: *"I think that this is a very hard choice. We think that the price is worth it"*

Miss Albright, what exactly was worth killing 500,000 children for? In November of 2000, Iraq began selling its oil exclusively in Euros. This was a direct attack on the dollar and on US financial dominance, and it wasn't going to be tolerated. In response, the US government with the assistance of the mainstream media, began to build up a mass propaganda campaign claiming that Iraq had weapons of mass destruction and was planning to use them.

In 2003, the US invaded and once they had control of the country, oil sales were immediately switched back to dollars. This is particularly noticeable as switching back to the dollar meant a 15% to 20% loss in revenue due to the Euro's higher value. It doesn't make any sense at all unless you take the Petro Dollar into account.

On 2nd March 2007, US General Wesley Clark said: *"So I came back to see him a few weeks later and by that time we were bombing in Afghanistan. I said: 'Are we still going to war with Iraq?' And he said 'Oh it's worse than that'. He said as he reached over on his desk and picked up a piece of paper and he said 'I just got this down from upstairs today* (meaning from the Secretary of Defense's Office), *this is a memo which describes how we are going to take out seven countries in five years, starting off with Iraq and Syria, Lebanon, Libya, Somalia, Sudan and finishing off Iran".*

Let's take a look at the events of the past decade and see if you see a pattern. In Libya, Gadaffi was in a process of organizing a block of African countries to create a gold-based currency called the "Dinar" which they intended to use to replace the dollar in that region. US and NATO forces helped to destabilize and topple the government in 2011 and after taking control of the region, US armed rebels executed Gadaffi in cold blood and immediately set up the Libyan Central Bank. Iran has been actively campaigning to pull oil sales off the dollar for some time now, and it has recently secured agreements to trade its oil in exchange for gold. In response, the US government with mainstream media assistance has been attempting to build international support for military strikes, on the pretext of preventing Iran from building a nuclear weapon. In the mean time they established sanctions which they admit are aimed at causing a collapse of the Iranian economy.

Syria is Iran's closest ally and they are bound by mutual defence agreements. The country is currently in the process of being destabilized with covert assistance from NATO and although Russia and China have warned the United States not to get involved, the White House has made statements in the past month indicating that they are considering military intervention. It should be clear that military intervention in Syria and Iran isn't just being considered – it is a foregone conclusion. Just as it was in Iraq and Libya, the US is actively working to create the context which gives them the diplomatic cover to do what they have already planned. The motive for these invasions and covert actions becomes clear when we look at them in their full context and 'connect the dots'.

Those who control the United States understand that if even a few countries begin to sell their oil in another currency, it will set off a chain reaction and the dollar will collapse. They understand that there is absolutely nothing else holding up the value of the dollar at this point, and so does the rest of the world. But instead of accepting the fact that the dollar is nearing the end of it's life-span, the "powers that be" have made a calculated gambit. They have decided to use the brute force of the US military to crush each and every resistant State in Africa and the Middle East.

That in itself would be bad enough, but what you need to understand is that this is *not* going to end with Iran.

China and Russia stated publicly and in no uncertain terms that they will *not* tolerate an attack on Iran or Syria.

Iran is one of their key allies, one of the last independent oil-producers in the region, and they understand that if Iran falls, then they will have no way to escape the dollar without going to war. And yet, the United States is pushing forward in spite of the warnings. What we are witnessing here is a trajectory which leads straight to the unthinkable. It is a trajectory which was mapped out years ago in full awareness of the human consequences.

But who was it that put us on this course? What kind of psychopath is willing to intentionally set off a global conflict which will lead to millions of deaths, just to protect the value of a fiat paper currency? It obviously isn't the President. The decision to invade Syria, Libya and Iran was made long before Obama had risen to the national spotlight, and yet, he is carrying out his duties just like the puppets who preceded him. So who is it that pulls the strings?

Often, the best answers to questions like this are found by asking another question *"Cui Bono?"* - *"Who Benefits?"*

Obviously, those who have the power to print the dollar out of thin air have the most to lose if the dollar were to fall, and since 1913, that power has been held by the Federal Reserve. The Federal Reserve is a private entity owned by a conglomerate of the most powerful banks in the world and the men who control those banks are the ones who pull those strings. To them, this is just a game. Your life, and the lives of those you love are just pawns on their chessboard. And like a spoiled four-year-old who tips over the board to the floor when he starts to lose, the powers that be are willing to start World War Three to keep control of the global financial system.

Remember that, when these wars accelerate and extend. Remember that, when your son, or your neighbor's son comes back in a flag-draped coffin. Remember that, when they point the finger at the new "bogeymen" because the madmen who are running this show, will take this as far as you allow them to take it.

So, how much time do we have left? It's a question which I hear constantly. But it is the wrong question. Asking how much time we have left is a passive posture. It is the attitude of a prisoner who is waiting to be taken out to a ditch and shot in the back of the head.

What are our chances? Can we change course? Also, the wrong question. The odds don't matter any more. If you understand what we are facing, then you have a moral responsibility to do everything in your power to alter the course we are on, regardless of the odds. It is only when you stop basing your involvement on the chances of your success, that success actually becomes possible. To strip the ill-begotten power from the financial elites and bring these criminal cartels to justice, will require nothing less than a revolution. The government is not going to save us. The government is completely infiltrated and corrupt to the core. Looking to them for a solution at this point is utterly naive.

There are three stages of revolution and they are sequential. Stage One is already underway.

Stage One is the ideological resistance. In this stage we have to actively work to wake up as many people as possible about what is happening and the direction we are headed. All revolutions originate from a shift in the mind-set of the population and no other meaningful resistance is possible without it. Success in this stage of the game can be measured by the contagion of ideas. When an idea reaches critical mass, it begins to spread on its own and seeps into all levels of society. In order to achieve that contagion, we need more people in this fight. We need more people speaking up, making videos, writing articles, getting this information onto the national and international stage, and we especially need to reach the military and the police.

Stage Two is civil disobedience, also known as Non-violent Resistance. In this Stage, you put your money where your mouth is, or more accurately, you withhold your money and your obedience from the government and you do everything in your power to bring the gears of the State to a halt. Practiced in mass, this method alone is often enough to bring a regime to its knees. However, if it fails at this stage, Stage Three is inevitable.

Stage Three is direct physical resistance. Direct physical resistance is the last resort and it should be avoided and delayed as long as possible and only invoked when all other options have been thoroughly exhausted. There are those who "talk tough" and claim that they will resist when the time comes, but what they fail to realize is that if you are inactive during the first two Stages, and save your efforts for the last resistance, you will fail.

When the Nazis in Germany were moving from door to door, dragging people out of their homes, that was the time to fight back physically, but due to the lack of ideological resistance and civil disobedience leading up to that moment, even an armed uprising would have likely failed at that point. An armed uprising can only succeed if the people have established an attitude of active resistance. And active resistance is only possible after their minds have broken free from the mainstream propaganda. If you want to fight back, then its now or never – you're not going to get another chance, and the stakes are far higher than they were in Nazi   Germany.

CLOSING GOOD NEWS

One of the major attacks mounted against you is to con you out of your money. Much of this is "government tax" on fuels which are burnt to provide energy - energy for transport, energy for heating, cooling, lighting, cooking, washing, drying, communications, entertainment, ... A major effort has been put into attempting to prevent you from finding out the simple fact that we are all surrounded by limitless energy and more importantly, preventing us from finding out how to tap into and use that energy. Tight control has been kept on educational establishments, publishing and mainstream news services. Patents have been suppressed, inventors harassed, intimidated and forced into silence by any available means.

The reality is that energy can be pulled from the air, using an aerial, and Hermann Plauson produced systems which provides more than 100 kilowatts of electrical energy and which needs no input whatsoever. There is nothing magical about this, as the energy comes from the ionosphere which the Sun continuously charges, so sorry folks, no magic, just practical engineering.

Energy can be pulled from the ground, as the Earth is a vast reservoir of energy. Energy can be taken from gravity by various methods, including just nudging weights sideways as they fall, powering a large wheel which turns a generator.

Energy can be drawn from changes in inertia, as just spinning a flywheel which drives a generator, allows that generator to power both the flywheel and other items of household equipment.

Ordinary, unmodified "petrol" generators can provide kilowatts of electrical power by splitting water into its component gasses and using those gasses to power the generator. Here, the generator both splits the water and powers the additional equipment.

It is possible to build a simple motor/generator which produces far more electrical power than is needed to make it run. Robert

Adams of New Zealand demonstrated this with quite small models which had a minimum of eight times more output power than input power, while more advanced models have outputs hundreds of times greater than the input power.

We are told (either tongue in cheek or based on complete ignorance) that permanent magnets can't do any useful "work". Dietmar Hohl has shown that anybody can build a simple rotor drum which is made to spin using just permanent magnets.

We are told that no electronics-driven transformer can output more than is used to drive it. Thane Heins has demonstrated that this is just not true, while by adding a permanent magnet to the transformer, Lawrence Tseung has shown that with just a simple iron frame, much more power can be drawn from the output than is needed to operate the frame.

The supposed limits taught by "educational" establishments are based on electric transfer methods in transformers running at low speeds, such as 50 or 60 cycles per second. However, if the transfer is made to be magnetic rather than electrical, and the cycle frequency exceeds 20,000 cycles per second and especially if the voltage is raised to a much higher level, then the output power from a simple, motionless device can be kilowatts more than the input power.

There are many, many ways to provide electrical power where no fuel is burnt, and where you do not have to pay for whatever energy you happen to draw from the system. There is no need for you to do any of this, but it is important that you understand that it can be done, and there is actually no need for you to be charged for every watt of electrical energy you choose to use.

Please download and read the eBook below. It is free and above all else, please understand fully that this technology has been suppressed for personal gain for more than a hundred years.

[free eBook]
http://www.free-energy-info.tuks.nl/PJKBook.html

FACTS YOU MAY NOT KNOW

1.   The UNITED STATES OF AMERICA was incorporated in London in 1783. The United States of America is a territory of Great Britain. The Colonists did not win the Revolutionary War. The British troops did not leave until 1796.

Republican v. Sweers, 1 Dallas 43; Treaty of Commerce, 8 Stat. 116; The Society for Propagating the Gospel & c. v. New Haven, 8 Wheat 464, Treaty of Paris (Peace), 8 Stat. 80, IRS Publication 6209, Articles of Association, October 20, 1774.

2.   King George III of England financed both sides of the Revolutionary War.

Treaty of Versailles, July 15, 1782; *Treaty of Paris (Peace),* 8 Stat. 80.

3.   The IRS is not a U.S. Government agency. It is a Debt Collection Agency of the International Monetary Fund (IMF).

Diversified Metal Products v. IRS, et. al., CV-93-405E-EJE,U.S.D.C.D.I., Public Law 94-564, Senate Report 94-1148 pg.5967, Bankruptcy Reorganization Plan No. 26, Public Law 102-391.

4.   The IMF is an agency of the United Nations (UN). — Black's Law, 6th Ed. pg. 816.

5. The U.S. has not had a Treasury since 1921. — 41 Stat. Ch. 214 pg. 654.

6.   New York City is defined in the Code of Federal Regulations (CFR) as the United Nations.

Rudolph Giuliani stated on C-Span that "New York City is the capitol of the World" and he is correct. 20 CFR Ch. 111, subpart B 422.103(b)(2).

7. No judicial courts, nor judges, have existed in America since 1789. Executive Administrators, not Judges, enforce Statutes and Codes.

FRC v. GE, 281 US 464, Keller v. PE, 261 US 428, 1 Stat. 138-178. See also the 11th Amendment. This was the abolishment of all inferior courts to hear cases of law or equity (this means that all courts below the "one supreme courts", not the U.S. Supreme Court.

8. You cannot use the U.S. Constitution to defend yourself because you are not a party to it. (use instead the Bill of Rights).

Padelford Fay & Co. v. The Mayor and Alderman of the City of Savannah, 14 Georgia 438, 520.

9. You own no property. Slaves cannot own property. Read the Deed to the property that you think you own. You are listed as a Tenant. — Senate Document 43, 73rd Congress, 1st. Session.

10. We are slaves and own nothing, not even who we think are our children.

Tillman v. Roberts, 108 So. 62; Van Koten v. Koten, 154 N.E. 146; Senate Document 43 and 73rd Congress 1st, Session' Wynehammer v. People, 13 N.R. REP 378, 481.

11. Great Britain is owned by the Vatican. — Treaty of Verona, 1213.

12. The Pope can abolish any law in the United States. — Elements of Ecclesiastical Law, Vol. 1, 53-54.

13. We are Human Capital. — See Executive Order 13037.

14. We are enemies of the State.

Trading with the Enemy Act or 1917 and 1933, October 6, 1917, under the Adr, Section 2, subdivision (c) Ch. 106 - Enemy defined "other than citizens of the United States..." March 9, 1933, Ch 106, Section 5, subdivision (b) of the Act of Oct. 6, 1917 (40 Stat. L. 411) amended as follows: "...any person within the United States." See H.R. 1491 Public law No. 1.

15. Your name when spelled in all capital letters is a corporation: A *Cestui Que Vie Trust.* — Cannon Law.

16. "The People" do not include you and me since our names are all Capital Letter fictional legal names. — Barron v. Mayor of City coundil of Baltimore, 32 U.S. 243.

17. A 1040 Form is for tribute paid to Great Britain (and the Vatican). — IRS Publication 6209 IMF decoding manual.

18. Everything in the "United States" is for sale: roads, bridges, schools, hospitals, water plants, prisons, airports, etc. (Who bought Klamath Lake in California?) — See Executive Order 12803.

19. It is not the duty of the police to protect you. Their job is to protect the Corporation and arrest Code breakers.

Sapp. v. Tallahassee, 348 S0.2d 363; Reiff v. City of Philadelphia, 477 F. Supp. 1262; Lynch v. N.C. Dept. of Justice, 376 S.E.2d 247.

20. The FCC, CIA, FBI, NASA and all the other alphabet gangs were never a part of the United States Government, even though the "U.S. Government" held shares of stock in the various agencies.

U.S. v. Strang, 254 U.S. 491; Lewis v. U.S., 6880 F.2d 1239.

LINKS FOR FURTHER INFORMATION

Rule By Secrecy - The Hidden History by Jim Marrs. This is a most remarkable and detailed account, naming names, stating events and revealing motives for most of history - a really spectacular work !!

pdf format: http://www.yourStrawman.com/Marrs.pdf
ePub format: http://www.yourStrawman.com/Marrs.epub
html format: http://www.yourStrawman.com/Marrs.htm

http://vimeo.com/71587843# **OUTLAWS-in-JUSTICE: USA Common Law officials, Anthony Williams, Hep Guinn, and others advancing a national organization to reestablish Common Law and Constitutional Law as the primary "law of the land" and "due process."** Additional comments: http://vimeo.com/71700258

http://www.yourStrawman.com/Emery.pdf **Seven Financial Conspiracies which have Enslaved the American People - the facts presented in a straightforward way**

http://www.youtube.com/watch?v=oCIhm0-H-O0&feature=youtu.be **The 'Fix The World' documentary which is an outline of current action being taken.** Alternative link: https://vimeo.com/68447896

http://www.yourStrawman.com/Bowie.pdf **The latest 2013 attack on world population with attempts to kill people such as yourself on a long-term basis.**

http://www.youtube.com/watch?v=lPTznFPh1MQ **The Fall of the Vatican, the Queen and the System - video details.**

http://www.yourStrawman.com/EireDesist.pdf **How Ireland has responded to bank foreclosures, opposing house**

repossessions, and some relevant responses:
http://www.oneworldchronicle.com/?p=12451

http://www.youtube.com/user/ThriveMovement A clear and comprehensive explanation of the present situation and what YOU can do about it.

http://www.youtube.com/watch?v=AXAnba23qV4 A 2013 video demonstrating that mortgages are fake and fraudulent and that the regulators have not the slightest intention of doing anything about it.

http://www.truth-now.net/case1.htm Australian Fakes: a video demonstrating that Australia has no lawful Courts, Police, Customs, Parliament, etc.

http://www.youtube.com/watch?v=Y7qXbv6U4YM Clear insights into the present situation, including why you personally are reading this

http://www.documentarywire.com/john-harris-its-an-illusion video lecture by John Harris

http://www.getoutofdebtfree.org sample letters for dealing with 'debt' issues

http://www.yourStrawman.com/VeronicaChapman.pdf very important information for those in the UK

http://www.thebcgroup.org.uk video British Constitution Group's seven video lectures

http://www.tpuc.co.uk John Harris' website 'The People's United Community'

http://www.raymondstclair.com Raymond St Clair's website with videos http://www.fmotl.com   The Freeman On The Land web site with a large amount of specific information

http://video.google.com/videoplay?docid=6399325693468031456 'Think Free' Part 1 - a top video presentation by Robert-Arthur Menard of Canada

http://video.google.com/videoplay?docid=6399325693468031456#docid=7257545709470673839 'Think Free' Part 2

http://thecrowhouse.com/Documents/mary-book.pdf   Mary Croft's eBook "How I Clobbered Every Bureaucratic Cash-Confiscatory Agency Known To Man"

http://educate-yourself.org/cn/Strawmanillusion02apr10.shtml The 'Educate-yourself.org' web site with video presentations

http://panacea-bocaf.org/honordishonor.htm   The Australian web site with links

http://video.google.com.au/videoplay?docid=3296715122664269567# 'Hijacking Humanity' - a great video presentation by Paul Verge of Canada

http://www.youtube.com/watch?v=YHZTjTmrgjI
                              Mary Croft interview Part 1
http://www.youtube.com/watch?v=alqgpuAwpzM&NR=1
                                                  Part 2
http://www.youtube.com/watch?v=8hqnaHNw_fo&feature=related   Part 3
http://www.youtube.com/watch?v=P9zxVMNmJsE&feature=related   Part 4
http://www.youtube.com/watch?v=iWnv66ERXiw&feature=related   Part 5
http://www.youtube.com/watch?v=BUD5f0MWnKo&feature=related   Part 6

http://www.zshare.net/audio/548937360de2ee12   A 143 Mb download file of an audio interview

http://www.archive.org/details/Michael_Badnarik   Michael Badnarik explains the American Constitution

http://web.archive.org/web/20060407062015/http://www.worldnewsstand.net/law/PLAY_BALL.htm   "The Commerce Game Exposed" - the present situation explained with emphasis on America

http://famguardian.org/TaxFreedom/Instructions/3.17QuitSocialSecurity.htm "Tax Freedom" - dealing with US taxes

http://video.google.com/videoplay?docid=-2550156453790090544# "Money As Debt" - a video on how (American) banks create money out of nothing

http://video.google.com/videoplay?docid=-515319560256183936# "The Money Masters" - a VERY long factual video explaining how we got where we are today

http://web.archive.org/web/20060206085143/www.worldnewsstand.net/law/REDEMPTION3.htm "The Application of Commercial Law"

http://www.free-energy-devices.com/Chapter15.pdf   The Historical Background of the Lies - how things developed in England and America

http://www.xtranormal.com/watch/11316911   This is a video which expresses the opinion of just one person. However, I am unable to fault anything said, other than to remark that I, personally, have not one shred of evidence of collusion on the part of some judges, even though I suspect it to be true.

http://www.lawfulrebellion.org **This is an important website with a good deal of relevant information**

http://www.youtube.com/watch?v=ElrXrE8AmIc **Video explaining how we and our children are being progressively poisoned.**

http://www.buildfreedom.com/tl/comliens.shtml **A website explaining a very powerful tool in defending yourself against unlawful attack: the 'lien'.**

http://www.yourStrawman.com/CommercialLiens.pdf **A pdf copy of that information:**

http://www.youtube.com/watch?v=sB4o3afM11w&feature=related **Video lecture by Robert M Nenard of Canada who is very knowledgeable.**

http://www.youtube.com/watch?v=n5cvEOpcSK0&feature=related   **Part 2**
http://www.youtube.com/watch?v=8oYhlasKrfY&feature=related   **Part 3**
http://www.youtube.com/watch?v=C2j2rMj-QPs&feature=related   **Part 4**
http://www.youtube.com/watch?v=0gGaFo7u50g&feature=related   **Part 5**
http://www.youtube.com/watch?v=kAVmGROLrpE&feature=related   **Part 6**
http://www.youtube.com/watch?v=LsRUKutNqP8&feature=related   **Part 7**
http://www.youtube.com/watch?v=RHXhntd4Wpg&feature=related   **Part 8**
http://www.youtube.com/watch?v=ALvNSsb-iWo&feature=related   **Part 9**

http://runnymede1215.wordpress.com **Website explaining the details of the physical strategies used against you by the courts.**

http://www.yourStrawman.com/Individualism.pdf A 150-page document explaining your present position and what you can do about it.

http://www.youtube.com/watch?v=PpUjl4LvQM8&feature=youtu.be&fb_source=mes An Irish house repossession stopped by the Constitution.

http://www.youtube.com/watch?v=_ae7h8FioX0 A 12-year old girl explains how banks rob ordinary people.

http://www.yourStrawman.com/DaCosta.pdf A letter laying out very clearly, the corruption of the legal system in Canada at the present time.

http://www.in5d.com/40-outrageous-facts-most-people-dont-know.html A clear statement of the present situation with supporting references.

http://www.pacalliance.us/perspectives/part1 The real situation explained in detail, especially for the people of America.

http://wakeup-world.com/2013/02/18/all-corporations-banks-and-governments-lawfully-foreclosed-by-oppt/ 2013

See the web page;

NationalLibertyAlliance.org

If you have any questions or comments feel free to email:

David Robinson
drobin88@comcast.net

Administrator
Unified Maine Common Law Grand Jury
for the Maine Republic Free State

Thanks for standing up to save our Republic.

Made in the USA
Las Vegas, NV
26 February 2022

44652045R00046